INSPIRATION THREE
for YOU *AND* YOUR FAMILY

"Life is not being religious but becoming religious, not being healthy but getting well, not being anything but becoming, not resting but working. We have not arrived, but shall do so; not yet is it finished, but it is in motion; the end is not yet, but we are on the way; not everything is bright and shining, but it is being polished."

—Martin Luther

"All men are overwhelmed with an inevitable calamity, from which they can never emerge unless they are extricated by the mercy of God."

—John Calvin

"I find it useful to be in such a state of suspense, wherein I know not what will be the next hour, but lean absolutely on His disposal, who knoweth and ruleth all things well."

—John Wesley

INSPIRATION THREE
Three famous classics in one book
Volume III

The Wisdom
of Martin Luther

The Wisdom
of John Calvin

The Wisdom
of John Wesley

Keats Publishing, Inc. New Canaan, Connecticut

Inspiration Three (Volume III)

A Pivot Family Reader
Pivot Family Edition published June 1973
Printed in the United States of America
Library of Congress Catalog Card Number: 73-80032

Pivot Family Reader paperbacks are published by
Keats Publishing, Inc., 212 Elm Street,
New Canaan, Connecticut 06840, U.S.A.

CONTENTS

With grateful thanks to my wife, Ann Reid Poling,
for her fine contribution to this book
in research and editorial assistance.

INTRODUCTION

IT IS IMPOSSIBLE for one to understand world history, western civilization, or Protestant Christianity without an awareness of Martin Luther, John Calvin, and John Wesley. These forceful religious personalities who lived in the 16th and 18th centuries continue to shape the attitudes and activity of millions of people in the 20th century. They were great men of faith, gifted in writing and speaking, determined in daily contact with others to bring a new grasp of the Christian life. They succeeded in different ways, to alter the course of history and to direct the affairs of Christian communities for hundreds of years.

Fortunately for us, not only did they have devoted followers who recorded their sermons, conversations, and speeches, but were themselves given to the written word. Luther poured enormous time and energy into a steady succession of books, pamphlets and letters. His great work was a German translation of the entire Bible. Calvin produced the monumental *Institutes of the Christian Religion* which all Christians regard as the most systematic account of Protestant theology and the first to be published among the reformers in 1559. His work, according to Calvin, "strictly follows the method of the Apostles' Creed, as being most familiar to all Christians. For the Creed consists of four parts, the first relating to God the Father, the second to the Son, the third to the Holy Spirit, the fourth to the Church." This remarkable effort, which was first published in French and forced Calvin into Swiss exile, was published before the Reformer was 30.

John Wesley did not share the same century with Luther and Calvin, but did extend and enlarge the vision of Christian witness in a global expression within the 1800's and after. Wesley's *Journal* is essential to the understanding of his evangelical zeal and influence, as well as the beginnings of world Methodism.

This volume is not intended as a text or even a dissertation of the life and work of these three men. Rather an introduction to their grasp of the Christian faith, an appreciation of them as men who shared humor and hope with others (and quite capable of error and injury), yet committed to a deeper, enduring knowledge of God. May our examination of them help us to look within our own lives and renew the fire and vision that gives life its purpose.

David Poling

MARTIN LUTHER

About
MARTIN LUTHER

Unless I am convicted by Scripture and plain reason—I do not accept the authority of popes and councils, for they have contradicted each other—my conscience is captive to the Word of God. I cannot and I will not recant anything, for to go against conscience is neither right nor safe. God help me. Amen.

—*Martin Luther*

JUST AS JESUS, a young and forthright Jew, would shock Judaism to its core, so Martin Luther, a young, sensitive Roman Catholic, would shatter the ancient traditions of the Christian community and be the singular force of reform, renewal, reformation and counter-reformation.

He was a personality of staggering contradictions and contrasts. The noted Reformation scholar and authority on Martin Luther, Roland Bainton, once wrote of him:

The man who thus called upon a saint was later to repudiate the cult of the saints. He who vowed to become a monk was later to renounce monasticism. A loyal son of

3

the Catholic Church, he was later to shatter the structure of medieval Catholicism. A devoted servant of the pope, he was later to identify the popes with Antichrist.

Martin Luther is the central figure of the great Protestant Reformation that included such personalities as John Calvin, Knox, Zwingli and perhaps a half dozen other religious leaders. Yet none of these matched the fire, brilliance and volcanic force that centered on this German monk. Luther today is a continuing source of fascination and interest to contemporary psychologists, historians, artists and theologians. While each of these academic disciplines have sought to pursue their own perspective and theory in the life of this reformer, he is primarily a religious force to more than 10 million Americans and many millions more overseas who are in the world Lutheran family.

To understand fairly this one-time Augustinian monk who lived in the fifteenth and sixteenth centuries, we must review his world, his culture and his stage. The rise of individualism sponsored by the Renaissance, the surge of nationalism and corruption within the established church were significant factors that shaped the ultimate events in the long drama which ended with the dividing of Christendom into Catholic and Protestant.

In Luther's mind, all these currents were reduced to religious problems and surely foremost among them was the question of personal salvation: what must I do to be saved?

Born in 1483, young Martin came from the most conservative religious element of the German population. Most biographers of Luther see in him a combination of the sophistication of the Renaissance with the primitive superstition of folk religion, firmly rooted in the mind of the peasantry. Above all else, Luther was possessed by a terror of the holy, a fear of the awesome majesty of God as well as His righteousness. This fear (which some critics felt was almost a psychological terror) centered on his personal sense of God's massive judgment on the sinner and his overwhelming dread. He was guilty before the seat of divine judgment.

An example of the religious folkways of the period—which were powerful in Luther's upbringing—can be seen in the way which Luther decided to become a monk and take the cowl. When he was twenty-two years old, still a university student preparing for the practice of law (here he was similar to Calvin in training), Luther was walking along the road of the outskirts of a small village. A sudden thunderstorm developed in the July afternoon and a bolt of lightning struck so close that the student was hurled to the ground. Trembling and shaken, he is said to have cried out, "St. Anne, help me! I will become a monk." While Luther was to have much stronger reasons for a divine vocation, he was not free from the perils and alarms that reigned over the daily lives of citizens of the sixteenth century.

In the volume, "Here I Stand," Bainton gives

the whole scene that battered the mind and actions of common people.

Certain elements even of old German paganism were blended with Christian mythology in the beliefs of these untutored folk. For them the woods and winds and water were peopled by elves, gnomes, fairies, mermen and mermaids, sprites and witches. Sinister spirits would release storms, floods, and pestilence, and would seduce mankind to sin and melancholia. Luther's mother believed that they played such minor pranks as stealing eggs, milk, and butter; and Luther himself was never emancipated from such beliefs. Many regions are inhabited, he said, by devils. Prussia is full of them, and Lapland of witches. In my native country on the top of a high mountain called the Pubelsberg is a lake into which, if a stone be thrown, a tempest will arise over the whole region because the waters are the abode of captive demons.

Shortly after the thunderstorm crisis, Luther put his affairs in order and without a word to his family, presented himself at the gates of an Augustinian monastery. He did not know that the final outcome of such a move would result, some twelve years later, on October 31, 1517, in his posting ninety-five theses on the church door at Wittenberg. It is this latter day which is observed around the world as the official beginning of the Protestant Reformation.

We have noted that Luther was not the only personality to be involved in the Reformation. It was not a solo event. In many countries of Europe the established Church (Roman Catholic) was in the process of disintegration. The new learning and the rise of individualism in arts, music and commerce—all fostered by the Renaissance period that preceded—played a heavy role in justifying the restrictions on Papal authority that were to come. The Papacy, in some instances, encouraged this shift; while in the case of Luther, the Papacy was to force the conflict and lose dramatically to a brilliant German priest.

The strategy taken by the Church during the fifteenth and sixteenth centuries was most heavy in politics, which had a bewildering cast in international affairs. The Church was responsible, indeed encouraged the rise of the young nation states. Papacy sought to assert itself against the national political figures and employed the vast conglomerate of states and kingdoms (Holy Roman Empire) as its secular arm. For Rome, Church and State should serve one master—the Papacy. The process was to evoke unexpected results.

The sociopolitical-cultural, and at times even military leadership, had, from medieval Pope to parish priest, caused a high degree of secularization of the system. One result was corruption.

Renaissance Popes and Cardinals were known for their worldly adventures and mistakes as much as for their piety and saintliness. Other church leaders were despots, rakes and spendthrifts.

All these currents were at work as Luther sought to work out his own salvation within the walls of the monastery. That these forces should converge while Luther was in a personal wrestling match over his own faith—and then be set free with such an explosive force that this obscure monk was thrust into the center of history so that millions honor him and use his name as the label for their Christian faith—is surely one of the supreme ironies of recorded history.

Indulgences—a highly complicated theory in which it was held that Christ and the saints had more merits than necessary for their own salvation and that, for a price, these merits could be made available for the forgiveness of someone's sins—was the key to the convergence of Luther's private theological struggle and the major events shaping world direction.

Luther's quest for the certainty of salvation had led him down many paths—his life at the monasteries of Erfurt and Wittenberg; his becoming a doctor of theology, followed by an intensive, brilliant study of Scripture, particularly the Psalms and Paul's letters to the Romans. It was in these studies that Luther came upon the idea and experience of "justification by faith." Not a new idea, as old surely as the

New Testament writings of St. Paul fifteen hundred years earlier; but new and powerful to the scholar-seeker who wrote:

> Then I grasped that the justice of God is that righteousness by which through grace and sheer mercy God justifies us through faith. Thereupon I felt myself to be reborn and to have gone through open doors into paradise.

This experience of grace is still the central tenet of Lutherans today. Dr. Luther believed that this should be normative for all men and out of this concept saw the folly of the practice of the church's selling indulgences and the people buying them. Selling indulgences, which popes, bishops, emperors and rulers had used as a means of fund-raising, not only contradicted Luther's new vision of the faith, but was corrupt and abused the church so much that it was hardly more than a raw scandal.

Luther spoke and wrote critically of indulgences. Finally, in 1517, the notorious Father Tetzel set up an indulgence sales booth near Wittenberg and proclaimed to all who would hear:

> As soon as the coin in the coffer rings,
> The soul from purgatory springs.

To the peasant mind it was an intriguing deal. To Luther, it was blasphemous. On the eve of All Saints Day, October 31, 1517, Luther posted for disputation (debate) on the church door his ninety-five theses attacking not only the abusive aspects of the sale of indulgences but some of the theory and justification for the practice. He was shooting at the source.

Although the ninety-five theses or "arguments" were not intended for mass distribution, they were printed and quickly spread across Germany. There began a long series of critical events—debates, pamphlet wars, appearances at Augsburg and Leipzig, as well as a great deal of lobbying among the various secular and ecclesiastical factions—that finally culminated in Luther's appearance at the Diet (Parliament) of the German nations at Worms. By now the question of indulgences had receded into the background for Dr. Luther. For in working out the implications of his new Biblical studies and the practice of indulgences, Luther found that he must challenge, of all things, the authority and infallibility of the Pope, Church Councils, and essential doctrinal questions. Even the sacraments were not excluded from his probe in study and library.

At the assembly at Worms the die was cast. Confronted with a stack of his vast writings, he was asked to repudiate them, to recant. Luther weighed the situation and then, in steady even tones, replied:

> Unless I am convicted by Scripture and plain reason—I do not accept the authority of popes and councils, for they have contradicted each other—my conscience is cap-

tive to the Word of God. I cannot and I will not recant anything, for to go against conscience is neither right nor safe. God help me. Amen.

For a year after the events at Worms, Luther lived in protected exile at Wartburg Castle where he continued to write and study. Here he began one of his greatest tasks—the translation of the Bible into German. Out of his own experience with the study of Scripture, he wanted to make the Holy Scriptures available to all men, not just the priest or scholar. Primacy of scripture as the norm for faith is one of the primary principles of the Reformation and is second only to the credo of "justification by faith," the rock for contemporary Lutherans.

While Luther chafed at Wartburg, though continuing to write, his ideas were taking concrete form and spreading throughout Germany. But violence and force erupted causing social and religious changes. Roland Bainton's comment sets the picture:

During his absence in 1521 and 1522 one innovation followed another with disconcerting rapidity. Priests married, monks married, nuns married. Nuns and monks even married each other. The tonsured permitted their hair to grow. The wine in the mass was given to the laity, and they were suffered to take the elements into their own hands. Priests celebrated the sacrament

without vestments in plain clothes. Portions
of the mass were recited in the German
tongue. Masses for the dead were discon-
tinued. Vigils ceased, vespers were altered,
images were smashed. Meat was eaten on
fast days. Endowments were withdrawn by
patrons. . . . All this could not escape the
eye of Hans and Gretel. Doctrine might go
over their heads, but liturgy was a part of
their daily religious life. They realized now
that the reformation meant something, and
this began to worry Luther.

A while later, Luther would marry and in his
discovery of domesticity, some robustness and
ribaldry would emerge. He had a huge capacity
for beer and an extremely biting wit and much
of his thought and comment would be taken
down by followers in "Table Talk." Yet ever
before him was his reluctant and final break
with Rome. Now the task of expounding his
views on faith would demand high priority. He
was not a systematic theologian and the expression of his ideas and thought is best found in
tracts, sermons, debates, scholarly works, and
hymns. His most famous hymns are "A Mighty
Fortress Is Our God" and "Away in a Manger."
Luther brought many talents to his task. Like
Wesley in a later century, he sang about his faith
as freely as he preached it. Classroom and pulpit
were joined. Music and theology, church and
state were never far apart. The great heritage
of Luther is today shared by nearly 75 million

people—nearly half of them in divided Germany. Another fourth are in the Scandinavian countries of Norway, Sweden, Denmark and Finland, while an estimated 9 or 10 million followers are in North America.

Although Lutherans were present in the young American colonies as early as the seventeenth century, it wasn't until the 1730's that the first large wave of German immigrants came to America, settling primarily in Pennsylvania. As war and depression hit Europe, there were small surges of Lutheran settlement but it was not until after the Civil War that the vast majority of Lutherans, from Germany and Scandinavia, came to the United States of America.

In addition to their Bibles and hymnals, these Lutheran arrivals brought with them their native tongue and national traditions. Early history of this group is a story of hyphenated development as German-Lutherans, Swedish-Lutherans, and Norwegian-Lutherans were established.

Even after these groups became assimilated and English was the favored language, Lutherans found themselves fragmented into a large number of different, and often competing groups. This fragmentation persists today but is slowly being overcome as theological differences are discussed and the general thrust toward ecumenical dialogue and union is felt among Lutherans.

The success of that movement can be judged by the fact that today some 95 percent of the Lutherans in the United States belong to three

major bodies—The Lutheran Church in America,
the American Lutheran Church, and the Lutheran Church-Missouri Synod. The other 5 percent are scattered among some ten other bodies.

   Luther would probably be embarrassed today
to know that there is a church named after
him—but those who call themselves by his name
wear it proudly and forcefully.

The Wisdom of
MARTIN LUTHER

MARTIN LUTHER wishes the reader sincere salvation!

[Holy Communion] Friend, stay away from this sacrament until you are a different person. Do not come because of the crowd, or the pope's law, or out of habit. . . . Alas, how far we are from Jerusalem! We have hardly begun to leave Babylon and act as if we were already home again. Everyone supposes himself a Christian and we have to give in. But a befitting faith or love they do not show.

We have to be coopers first and make new barrels before the new wine harvest begins. I do not like it that the reforms do not go forward, but my complaint is that they cannot do so. Where are the men that can carry on? First we must have the right men for the new freedom. One cannot compel anyone to faith, but must let the gospel call those whom it will. I see, however, that Satan is about, making the sacrament so common, yes even more so than the Pope—rather than that men are being made into Christians who need the sacrament.

This is the worthiest preparation: when a person is worst prepared. That is, when he knows himself to be entirely unsaved, poor, and in need of grace, and does not permit himself to think that he is worthy or is offering God a pure heart. For the heart of man is perverted, evil, and unfathomable. Therefore, the true and enduring test is whether a person finds himself vain and empty, burdened with many evil lusts, and not empty of all salvation and righteousness. Then he should diligently and ardently long for God's grace and mercy and have no doubt that he will receive it.

This is our doctrine, that bread and wine do not avail, indeed, not even the body and the blood in bread and wine. I will say more: Christ on the cross with all his sufferings and death does not help, even if this is meditated upon in the most ardent, heartfelt manner. Something else must be there. What is it? The Word, the Word, the Word makes it effective! For though Christ were given and crucified for us a thousand times, it would all be in vain, if God's Word did not come and say at the distribution of the elements: This shall be yours. Take it for your own!

We poor mortals, who live by the five senses, require at least an outward sign besides words, around which we can gather, and to which we can hold. Therefore Christ has affixed to his testament the noblest seal and sign: that is his true flesh and blood in bread and wine.

I would like to say, also, that I cannot believe that God's son had become a man and had bounded his majesty in the confines of a woman's body and thereupon let himself be crucified. There is no rational being so lowly but that it would not rather believe that merely bread and wine are present, rather than Christ's flesh and blood is hidden therein. But if we handle our faith in such a way that we ever read into Scripture our own puny ideas, and dare not see anything but what is at the level of the masses and common sense, then no article of faith can survive.

[Preaching] If others want to listen, the doors are open. If one would preach to the intellectuals and toss out real sermon masterpieces, the common folk would be as bewildered as a cow before a new gate. And even if they would say, "Aye, he preached splendidly", when one would ask them, "What did he say?" they would answer, "I don't know."

One does not have only gold and silver vessels in the tabernacle, but also copper and iron ones. If someone can teach simply from the Catechism, he is a fine preacher. My advice would be that one should simply read the text, a chapter from the Bible, and then pray and exhort the people to a disciplined life. For the world as it is, that would be the best preaching. But for the sake of troubled consciences, one must also preach the gospel to comfort them. The crowd wants a Moses with horns.

It would be a good thing, therefore, if there
were fewer saint's days, since in our times the
works done on those days are for the greater
part worse than those done on work days, what
with the idling about, gluttony, drunkenness,
gambling and other evil deeds. But worse than
that, the mass and the sermon are heard without
edification, and the prayer is said without faith.
It has almost gotten to the point where we think
it is enough to watch the mass with our eyes,
hear the preaching with our ears, and say the
prayers with our mouths. It has reached the
stage that men try to gain heaven by outward
acts! . . . Of course, the greatest blame in this
matter attaches to the bishops and priests, or
those to whom the work of preaching is entrusted, because they do not preach the gospel
and teach the people how they ought to watch
the mass, listen to the sermon, and pray.

The sermon ought to be nothing less than the
proclamation of the testament. But who can hear
it if nobody preaches it? Those who should be
preaching it do not know it themselves. That
is why sermons ramble off into good-for-nothing
fables, and thus Christ is forgotten. We are in
the position of the man in II Kings 7; we see
our riches but do not enjoy them. Ecclesiastes
also speaks of this: This is a great evil, when
God gives a man riches and does not let him
enjoy them. And so we see countless numbers
of masses, and yet we do not know whether
the mass is a testament, or whether it is this

thing or that thing, just as if it were any other ordinary good work in itself. O God, how utterly blind we are! But where this is rightly preached, it must be diligently heard, grasped, retained, pondered often, and faith must be strengthened against every temptation of sin, whether past or present or to come.

This preaching should induce sinners to grieve over their sins and should kindle within them a longing for the treasure. Therefore, it must be a grievous sin not to listen to the gospel, and to despise such a treasure and so rich a feast to which we are bidden. But it is a much greater sin not to preach the gospel and to allow so many people who would gladly hear it perish; for Christ has strictly commanded that the gospel and this testament be preached, that he does not even wish the mass to be celebrated unless the gospel be preached.

For this reason it is dreadful and horrible to be a bishop, pastor and preacher in our times, for no one knows this testament any longer, not to mention that they ought to preach it, although this is their highest and only duty and obligation. They will certainly have to account for the many souls who perish because of such feeble preaching!

I believe that it has now become clear that it is not enough or in any sense Christian to preach the works, life and words of Christ as historical facts, as if the knowledge of these would suffice for the conduct of life; yet this is the fashion among those who must today be regarded as our best preachers. . . . Now there are not a few who preach Christ and read about him that they may move men's affections to sympathy with Christ, to anger against the Jews, and such childish and effeminate nonsense. Rather ought Christ to be preached to the end that faith in him be established that he may not only be Christ—but Christ for you and me, and what is said of him be effectual in us. Such faith is produced and preserved in us by preaching.

Anyone, therefore, who has a burdened and sorrowful conscience prays here for grace and forgiveness of sins, that is, for the strength of the name, the kingdom, and the will of God. This petition serves those who are conscious of their sins. May everyone acknowledge the need which he feels! I do not do enough in my office of preaching. You, burgomaster, captain, prince, husband, wife, you do not do enough in your office either. I do not do enough for my neighbor. Therefore, we must pray daily for forgiveness of sins.

The round halo which is painted around the heads of saints is around the heads of parents, too. The golden halo or diadem came from the heathen. Later it became a garland, then flowers were added, and now it has become a bishop's mitre. This Word of power is painted around the heads of parents.

[Scripture]: No one really understands Scripture unless it comes into his house, that is, he experiences it. One must look at the words as if they had just been written yesterday. One must understand the words rightly and feel them in the heart.

If the passage is obscure, I consider whether it treats of God's law or grace, of wrath or forgiveness of sins, wherever it fits best. Thereby I have often understood the most obscure passages because God has a different doctrine in law and gospel. That is my first rule in translating. The second is that I ask others who know languages better than I do whether the grammar supports the meaning which seems closest to the mark.

[The Luther Bible]: It is clearer and surer in many passages than the Latin, and where careless printers don't spoil it, the German language now possesses the best Bible.

O, that God would allow all the expositions, mine and those of all teachers, to perish, and that every Christian would simply take the plain Scriptures as God's Word! Therefore, get into the Bible, dear Christians, for here God dwells alone in Zion. Amen.

Latin letters hinder good German greatly. One cannot ask the Latin how to talk German properly, as the donkeys do it, but one has to ask the mother in her house, the children in the

street, the common man in the marketplace and
observe how they speak and so translate. If they
can understand you, then you know you are
talking German.

[Love]: We must have Christian love and out
of love do to each other as God has done for
us through faith. Here, dear friends, much is
lacking. I do not see this love in anyone, and
mark well that you have not been grateful to
God for such a rich treasure. Dear friends, the
kingdom of God, which we are, is not in words
but in deeds. God does not want listeners and
talkers, but followers in love. It is not that each
one must do what he has a right to do, but what
is helpful for the weak brother.

Love I say, is a fruit of faith, which has been
preached much. All my books are directed toward active faith and love. If you will not love
each other, then God will send a great plague
upon you. Act accordingly.

Christ never gave any other commandment
than that of Love, because he intended that this
commandment be the test of His disciples and
of true believers. For if good works and love
do not blossom forth, it is not genuine faith,
the gospel has not yet gained a foothold and
Christ is not yet rightly known.

Paul cites the example of Christ, and teaches
that we should bear with others who are weak,
even including open sinners and those who have

disgusting habits. We must not cast them off, but be patient with them until they reform. That is what Christ did in our own case, and continues to do day by day; for He bears with the many shortcomings and evil habits, as well as all sorts of imperfections on our part, yet He never fails to help us.

[Marriage]: Now there are three kinds of love: false love, natural love, and married love. False love is that which seeks its own, as a man loves money, possessions, honor, and women taken outside of marriage and against God's command. Natural love is that between father and child, brother and sister, friend and relative, and similar relationships. But over and above all these is married love, that is, a bride's love, which glows like a fire and desires nothing but the husband. She says, "It is you I want, not what is yours: I want neither your silver nor your gold; I want neither. I want only you. I want you in your entirety or not at all." All other kinds of love seek something other than the loved one: this kind wants only to have the beloved's own self completely.

I have a pious and faithful wife who won't spoil anything for me. Ah, dear God, marriage is not just a natural thing, but a gift of God, the sweetest, most chaste life, better than any celibacy.

It is a great thing, this companionship of man and wife.

There has been such a thing as marriage itself ever since the beginning of the world, and it also exists amongst unbelievers to the present day. Therefore no grounds exist on which the Romanists can validly call it a sacrament of the new law and a function solely of the church. The marriages of our ancestors were no less sacred than our own, nor less real among unbelievers as believers.

Of truth no work is more wonderful in all of nature than begetting children. It is the highest work next to worship. If Adam had remained in the state of innocence, this work would have been holy and honorable and there would have been no shame which arises from sin, so that man and wife need to hide. It must be so and not otherwise. Your body needs it; God wills it so and makes it so. Away with such thoughts and enjoy it. Of course, a man has to control himself and not make a filthy sow's sty of his marriage. Pray for me that God may sanctify and bless this estate.

[The Peasant Revolt]: To Lords, Clerics and Princes: We have no one to thank more for such trouble and tumult than you, who do nothing more in ruling than cheat and tax, live in haughty pomp, until the common man cannot bear it any longer. The sword is at your necks. You think you still sit firmly in the saddle, and they cannot unseat you. Such certainty and stubborn arrogance will break your necks, you'll see it happen. If the peasants do not do it, then others will. Though you should defeat them all, they would still not be defeated. God will raise others. For he will strike you down. It is not the peasants, my lords, who are against you, but God himself.

Some blame the gospel and say it is the fruit of my doctrine. Well, go ahead with such slanders, my lords. You must bear witness that I have taught with all propriety, combated revolt mightily, and exhorted all subjects to be obedient even to a tyrannical and raging government. If now God intends to punish you, what can I or my gospel do about it?

[To Peasants]: Yes, you say you will let the lords live and keep enough of their possessions. Let him believe that who will. I won't. Whoever dares such injustice as seizing the power of the government will also hold back in little things. If the wolf devour a whole sheep, he will also devour an ear.

I am concerned that certain prophets of murder are come among you, who would like to use you to become lords of the world, and care not if they lead you into danger of life, property, honor and soul. Look to your freedom lest you run to escape the rain and fall into the water.

With God's help I will prepare for death and

await my new masters, the robbers and murderers, who say they will harm no one. O, what lovely innocence! How beautifully the devil and his henchmen dress themselves.

There are two kingdoms, the one is God's Kingdom, the other the world's kingdom; so often have I written that, I wonder that they don't know it yet. The worldly authority, however, cannot and should not be merciful in its own office. Whoever would mingle the two would put God's wrath in God's kingdom and mercy in the world's kingdom—that would be putting the devil in heaven and God in hell. Not so, dear friends. If one has earned wrath in the worldly kingdom, then one must submit and suffer the penalty, or humbly plead for pardon.

If they had followed my counsel when this revolt began, and quickly hit one or a hundred peasants on the head, then many thousands would have been saved. That would have been a necessary mercy.

There is much that is weak in women.

[Communion of Saints]: Through this congregation on earth the Holy Spirit speaks, because he has not yet gathered all his Christendom, nor dispensed forgiveness. Rather he fetches us by the Word and bestows, increases and strengthens faith so that he may finally sanctify us eternally, which is what we now await in faith.

I, too, am a doctor, as learned and experienced as any other, yet like a child, each morning and whenever I have the time, I still repeat the Ten Commandments, the Creed, the Lord's Prayer. And I still have to read and study daily and do not measure up as I would like and so remain a pupil of the catechism.

He who wishes to dwell in a country has to know its laws and keep them, whether he believes—God grant it—or is at heart a knave and a rascal.

It is better that learning should collapse rather than religion, if it will not serve Christ.

[Ark of Noah]: I would have died on that ship!

Dear brother, be not proud, or too confident and certain that you know Christ well. For this is not something which can be learned completely, nor can one boast of his knowledge. It is an art which would be our teacher while we remain the pupils.

No religion is so foolish to human reason and so preposterous as the Christian.

[To a Critic]: God has made everything depend on a basic conception which you do not have in your philosophy—it is faith. On this basic concept rests all that cannot be seen or understood, and if anyone would make it understandable and obvious, as you do, he will har-

vest for his trouble only worry and tears as you
do. The Lord has said that he would dwell in
clouds and has surrounded his Mystery with
darkness. It does not matter what anyone else
thinks.

We cannot be perfect as the preachers and
monks dream. Rather perfection is seeing first
that the doctrine is right and then that one's life
is directed accordingly. Even if life does not
measure up, as it could not do anyway, that does
not matter. Only one must strive for it.

To love is nothing other than to wish another
heartily what is good. If there were no one who
erred, whom would you love? The love cannot
exist where there are none who do not always
stumble and fall and sin.

Faith is the active righteousness of works and
works are the passive righteousness of faith.

All who teach that there is any other service
of God needful for salvation than the First Commandment, namely to fear, love, and trust in
God, are nothing but unchristian.

From the beginning of the world this key
heresy of freedom of the will and the merit of
good works has continued. And this feud will
never end. The explanation is this: reason is not
able to surrender to faith alone. If anyone would
believe solely and purely in God's Word, it must

be the work of the Holy Spirit in his heart. Out of its own powers human spirit cannot do so. No matter what one says, human nature holds on to the merit of good works.

Now there are four kinds of men. The first who need no law, of whom St. Paul says in I Timothy 1 "For the righteous man no law is laid down." Such men do willingly what they know and can, because they alone are distinguished for their firm confidence that God's favor and grace rests upon them in all things. The second class of men wants to abuse this freedom, put false confidence in it, and grow lazy. The third class are wicked men, who are always ready to sin. They must be restrained like wild horses and dogs by spiritual and temporal laws, and where this does not help, they must be put to death by the temporal sword. The fourth class are those who are still lusty and childish in their understanding of such faith and spiritual life, and they must be coaxed like young children, enticed with external, definite concomitant adornment, with reading, praying, fasting, singing, churches, decorations, organs and all those things commanded and observed in monasteries and churches, until such time as they too learn to know the teachings of faith.

Some people think that going on a pilgrimage is a precious good work. This is not true. It is a very small good work. Frequently it is evil and misleading, for God has not commanded it. But God has commanded that a man should care for his wife and children, perform the duties of a husband, and serve and help his neighbor. Today a man makes a pilgrimage to Rome and spends, fifty, maybe a hundred gulden; something nobody commanded him to do. He permits his wife and child, or his neighbor at any rate, to suffer want back home. And yet the silly fellow thinks he can gloss over such disobedience and contempt of the divine commandment with this self-assigned pilgrimage, which is really nothing but impertinence or a delusion of the devil.

Life is not being religious but becoming religious, not being healthy but getting well, not being anything but becoming, not resting but working. We have not arrived, but shall do so; not yet is it finished, but it is in motion; the end is not yet, but we are on the way; not everything is bright and shining, but it is being polished.

[Little could his parents have dreamt what a warrior Luther was to be in fighting corruption in the "Church militant here on earth!"] "Who foresaw this in the stars? Who could have told my career beforehand?" he questioned years after, when the Holy Roman Empire was seething with the ferment he had raised.

"My mother, father and grandfather were all peasants," he said frankly.

[Concerning discipline]: The apple must be beside the rod. Children should not be punished for taking trifling things like cherries, apples, pears, nuts, as though they were serious matters. My parents dealt with me so severely that I was completely cowed.

I have been a beggar of crumbs and have taken my bread at the door, especially at Eisenach, my favourite town.

It is my advice that the books of Aristotle, *Physics, Metaphysics, The Soul* and *Ethics,* be entirely removed from the curriculum. No one has ever understood Aristotle's meaning, and yet this study is kept up to waste time and overburden the soul. . . . There is no worse book than his *Ethics,* which goes directly contrary to God's grace and Christian virtue. . . . But I would gladly allow Aristotle's book on logic and his *Poetics* to be kept, at least in an abbreviated form.

He who wants to learn true philosophy must read Cicero: he has written more than all the Greeks, and has read all the books of the Greeks.

To pray well is to study well.

Music is a gift of God, not a human thing. She drives away the devil, makes people cheerful. One forgets anger, unchastity, pride and other vices. She is close to theology. Those who sing are cheerful fellows, who shake off their

worries and are not bothered by the noise of
the marketplace.

Music is the art of the prophets: it is the only
one which, like theology, can calm the agitations
of the soul, and put the devil to flight.

I have always loved music. . . . Whosoever
hath skill in it is of a good kind fitted for all
things.

Singers drive away sorrow by their singing.

In the time of peace music reigns.

I was called to this vocation by the terrors
of Heaven, for neither willingly nor by my own
desire did I become a monk, but surrounded by
the terror and agony of a sudden death I vowed
a forced and irrevocable vow.

The sad, austere life with my parents when
young was really the cause of my fleeing to the
cloister.

If Augustine went straight to Heaven, from
the walls of an Abbey, I too ought to have done
so. All my brethren would give me this testimony. I fasted, I watched, I mortified myself,
I practised all the monastic severities till I made
myself absolutely ill.

[A Florentine hospital]: Here the patients were

supplied with the best food and drink, and tended by diligent servants and skillful physicians. The painted bedsteads were covered with clean linen. When a patient is brought in his clothes are taken off and given to a notary to keep honestly. Then they put a white bedgown on him and lay him between the clean sheets, and two physicians are brought at once. Servants fetch food and drink in clean glass vessels, and do not touch the food even with a finger, but offer it to the sufferer on a tray. Honourable matrons, veiled, serve the poor all day long, without making their names known, and at evening return home.

[Visiting Rome]: Hail, Holy City. Thrice holy art thou, in whom the blood of the martyrs has been poured out!

I would not have missed seeing Rome for a hundred thousand florins. I should ever have been uneasy lest I might have done injustice to the Pope.

Upon a Doctor (of Theology) it is incumbent, according to his oath of office, to explain the Scriptures to all the world and to teach every one.

[A letter to the Archbishop of Mainz]:
Venerable Father in God, most illustrious prince, vouchsafe to cast a favourable eye on me who am but dust and ashes, and to receive

my request with pastoral kindness. There is circulated throughout the country in the name of your grace and lordship the Papal indulgence for the erection of St. Peter's at Rome. I do not so much object to the declarations of the preachers of the indulgence as to the erroneous idea entertained of them by the poor, simple and unlearned, who are everywhere openly avowing their fond imaginations on the subject. This pains me and turns me sick.

If the work be of God, who shall prevent it . . . if it be of man, who shall promote it?

[A letter to the Pope]:

I cast myself at your feet with the offer of myself and all that is in me. Pronounce the sentence of death or life, call, recall, approve, disapprove, I acknowledge your voice to be the spirit of Christ Who reigns and speaks in you. If I have deserved death I shall not flinch from dying.

Rome now laughs at good men: in what part of the Christian world do men more freely make a mock of the best bishops than in Rome, that true Babylon?

I do not see in what way I can escape the verdict intended against me except by the aid of the prince. . . . To Rome . . . why the Pope himself would not be in safety there. They have paper and ink enough and scribes without number, and can easily write in what I have erred.

If I must die what a scandal I shall be to my dear mother and father.

I have preached no new doctrine. It is to be found in the Bible, in the writing of the Fathers and the Canons. . . . I am not conscious of having said anything that is contrary to Holy Scripture, the Fathers of the Church, or the decretals of the Pope. Why not submit the whole dispute to the judgment of the University of Paris?

There is no news here, except that the town is full of talk about me, and everybody wants to see the man who, like a second Herostratus, has kindled such a flame. . . . I go to be sacrificed for them and for you, if God so will. For I will rather die . . . than revoke anything that it was right for me to say.

[To the Pope]: My writings have been published far and wide, they cannot be recalled. . . . They whom I have resisted, most blessed Father, have brought infamy on the Roman Church among us in Germany. . . . They blame me who have contended with such monsters. Before God and all men I attest that I have never wished, nor do I wish today, to touch in any way or plot against their power and that of the Roman Church. . . . The power of the Church is above everything in Heaven and Earth except Jesus Christ.

If you try to ride to Heaven on the Pope's wax and parchment your carriage will soon break down and you will fall into Hell.

I declare, that neither Pope, bishop, nor any man, has the power to impose the smallest matter on a Christian, except by his own consent.

[To Pope Leo]: Father Leo, beware how you listen to those sirens who make you no mere man, but a demigod, so that you can command and exact whatever you will. It will not be so always nor will you prevail; you are a servant of servants. . . . Let them not deceive you who pretend that you are Lord of the World.

Never since the beginning of the world has Satan spoken so shamelessly against God as in this Bull. It is impossible for anyone who accepts it, and does not contest it, to be saved.

I will go [to the Imperial Diet of Worms] if I am carried sick in my bed. I am called of the Lord when the Emperor calls me. Further, if they intend violence, as is very likely, my case is to be commended to the Lord. The same Lord lives and reigns Who preserved the three youths in the fiery furnace of Babylon, and if He does not choose to preserve me my head is a very small thing in comparison with Christ, Who was slain with the utmost ignominy. . . . I trust only that the Emperor will not begin his reign by shedding innocent blood, I would rather be murdered by them of Rome.

It is a question of faith and the salvation of souls. That I may answer without injury to the divine word or peril to my soul.

Do Thou, my God, stand by me against all the world's wisdom and reason. Not mine, but Thine, is the cause.

Unless I am convicted of error by the Scriptures, or by powerful reason, neither can I nor will I dare to retract anything, for my conscience is bound to God's word. Here stand I: I can do no other! God help me, amen.

Had I a hundred heads, they should all have been cut off before I would recant a word!

One has to ask the mother in her home, the children in the street, the common man in the market place, and to look at their mouths to see how they speak, and thence to interpret it [the Bible] to oneself, and so to make them understand. I have often laboured to do this, but have not always succeeded in hitting off the meaning.

Suddenly and unexpectedly God has taken me captive in the bonds of matrimony. . . . My Lord, Catherine and I beg that you will send us as soon as possible at my charge a keg of the best Torga beer you can find, in order that my father and mother and good friends may be joyful at the feast. . . . It must be seasoned and cool that it may taste well. If it is not good I shall punish you by making you drink it all yourself. I hope that you and your Audi will not stay away, but will appear in merry mood.

You see how rich the Christian is, since, even should he desire it, he is unable to forfeit his salvation, no matter how many sins he may commit, unless indeed he refuses to believe. No sin but unbelief can bring him damnation. Sin boldly, but believe boldly too.

God is above mathematics. Christ's body is in the sacrament as the sword is in the scabbard.

We left Marburg with the hope that as they had conceded all the Christian articles, and had receded from their former error concerning the Holy Sacrament they would in time completely unite with us.

I was lately looking out of my window when I beheld two wonderful sights. First I saw the stars and God's fair bright firmament, but nowhere any pillars on which the Master Builder had poised this lofty frame; yet the heavens did not fall in, and the firmament stood quite fast. But there are some who search for such pillars and would anxiously grasp and feel them, and, because they cannot do this, fear and tremble lest the heavens should fall. The other spectacle

I saw was a great, dense cloud floating over us, so charged and burdened that it might be likened to a mighty sea, though I could perceive no coffer in which it was enclosed; and yet it fell not, but, greeting us with a black frown, passed on.

[At the death of his little daughter Elizabeth]: 'Tis wonderful how sick at heart her loss has made me. I feel like a woman, so great is my agitation. I could never believe that a man's soul could be filled with such tenderness.

I would have disputed with God [concerning the sacrifice of Abraham to God]. God must be kinder to us, and speak more gently to us. Neither Kate nor I would pluck the eye out, nor knock the head off our child, and neither will God. He gave His only Son to make us trust him.

Rejoice, O young man, in thy youth, and let thy heart be of good cheer. . . . Joy and good humour in honour and seemliness is the best medicine for a young man, yea, for all men. I, who have hitherto spent my life in mourning and sadness, now seek and accept joy wherever I can find it.

My Lord Kathe [Luther's wife] . . . rides about, cultivates the fields, raises and buys cattle, brews beer and the like. At the same time she has begun to read the Bible, and I have promised her fifty florins if she finishes before Easter.

There is no union, no society, more beautiful to look upon, more gentle, more felicitous in itself, than a well-assorted marriage. It is perfectly delightful to see a well-assorted pair living together in peace and mutual love.

The ancients have described four principal virtues: Moderation which preserveth the body, Justice which maintaineth the state and commonwealth, Courage, or manliness, which resisteth and defendeth, and Wisdom which governeth all.

The Bible is like a fair and spacious orchard, wherein all sorts of trees do grow, from which we may pluck divers kinds of fruits; for in the Bible we have rich and precious comforts, learnings, admonitions, warnings, promises, and threatenings.

What is the difference between the Bible and other books?

The Holy Scripture . . . is full of divine gifts and virtues. The books of the Heathen taught nothing of Faith, Hope and Love, nay, they knew nothing at all of the same.

What should we seek in the Holy Scripture?

Well and rightly to learn to know Christ, for he is therein very friendly and familiarly pictured unto us.

Where great wealth is, there are all manner of sins; for through wealth cometh pride; through pride, dissension; through dissension, wars; through wars, poverty, and through poverty, great distress and misery.

Wealth is the most insignificant thing in the world, the meanest gift in God's power to bestow on man. What is it compared with the Word of God? The Almighty usually gives riches to rude donkeys on whom he bestows nothing else.

War is one of the greatest plagues that can afflict humanity; it destroys religion, it destroys states, it destroys families, any scourge, in fact, is preferable to it.

I do believe that I am that great trumpet which prefaces and announces the coming of the Lord. Therefore, weak and failing as I may be, and small as may be the sound that I can make this world hear, my voice rings in the ears of the angels in Heaven, who will take up the strain after us and complete the solemn call.

Ah, loving God, come at once: I wait continually for that day, (the end of the world) when early in the morning . . . I see a very clear morning sky. For I think swiftly out of the morning redness will come a thick black cloud, out of which will issue three flashes of lightning, afterwards there will come a clap, and in a moment will overwhelm Heaven and earth. . . . I am of the opinion, after or about Easter, when the year is at the finest and fairest, early at the rising of the sun, the element will be gloomy with earthquakes and thunderings about an hour or a little longer; then the secure people shall say, "Look, thou fool, hast thou never heard it thunder?"

To the gracious lady Catherine Luther, who torments herself far too much. You alarm yourself as if God was not all-powerful and as if He could not make Doctor Martins by the dozen if the first should be drowned . . . or perish in any other manner. I have One that takes care of me better than you do, or any of the angels could do, One who is seated at the right hand of God Almighty.

Who hath believed my word shall never see death.

JOHN CALVIN

About
JOHN CALVIN

> Protestantism had produced its prophets, preachers and theologians, but it had not yet produced an ecclesiastical statesman; an architect on earth of that city whose builder and maker is God. In Calvin he appeared.
>
> from The Protestant Tradition
> by J. S. Whale

IN EVERY GREAT religion of the world we find a major personality at the beginning. Not a committee, group, or assembly, but a person. For the Presbyterians and members of the Reformed tradition, John Calvin is the source and inspiration for their special understanding of the Christian faith. Just as Martin Luther is the key to the Lutheran experience, John Wesley to the Methodists, Moses to the Jews, Calvin is the mover and shaker of Presbyterian belief. Apart from Calvin, the Presbyterian and Reformed Churches would not exist.

But first we need to catch the drama that poured so much excitement and emotion into

the affairs of church and society that made up
the 16th century. The Christian Church, under
the direction of the Popes and Councils in Rome,
had governed the faithful within the medieval
framework for more than a thousand years. The
Holy Roman Empire, interwoven with the life
of the Church, ruled most of Western Europe.
But signs of change, advance and upheaval were
evident in the lives of citizens everywhere.

First of all, as the Middle Ages drew to a close,
there was a vast moral compulsion for change.
Church and State had become tired, and in some
instances, enmeshed in decay and corruption.
The great universities seeded an intellectual
change expressed in terms of humanism not
subject to the doctrines of the Church or the
expectations of the State. A third major force
was the anti-clerical mood that had been building for decades. A frank distrust for priests and
monks was evident. The vast land holdings of
monasteries and bishops annoyed the common
people. Such a learned philosopher and Roman
Catholic as Erasmus noted that the monks were
"almost universally hated."

Dr. J. S. Whale, scholar and historian, notes
that mystical and pietistic movements began to
spring up. These groups in Holland and Germany were very anti-institutional and critical
of the outward forms of Christianity. They
sought a return to the simple message and life-
style of the New Testament.

Nationalism was also at work. Indeed, Luther
in his break with the powers of Rome aimed

his appeal at the consciences of German princes who were gaining in political power and national independence. Economics means a shift in the balance of power: Europe was turning away from an agrarian culture built on feudalism, to the money economy of the new industrial society. Capitalism began in the sixteenth century and Calvin, with Luther, were at the source of this mighty spring. The bankers, traders and new mercantile class were to form the broad base of support that gave the sixteenth century reformers their congregations. These were the same classes that sought the culture of the university, the political independence of the state, and the individual freedom of the citizen. Calvin was to become their spokesman. The Bible would become their guide.

Calvin was dependent on the frontier work of Martin Luther. Luther broke with Rome and the Roman Catholic Church in 1517, Calvin, not until 1533. He was a second-generation reformer and his most powerful contribution, *The Institutes of the Christian Religion,* would not appear until 1536. Born and educated in France, young Jean was trained in law. At twenty-four years of age he fled Paris after admitting his conversion to the cause of the Reformers, Luther in particular. For Calvin the study of scripture was the turning point and the letters of St. Paul, the divine trigger. The Bible was the whole reason for the Reformed tradition, he claimed, and the sovereignty of God the highest recognition that a believer could profess.

Calvin made his way to Geneva, Switzerland, where Protestants were both powerful and free. The Swiss communities enjoyed a great deal of autonomy and offered French and German refugees a haven during the storms which swirled around the Reformation events. At first Calvin did not persuade either Church or city that he had all the answers to their theological and political problems. He wanted a true spiritual reformation to shape the lives of the whole citizenry. They were not ready for his theocratic politics or his sense of discipline in the life of the congregation. Suffering temporary banishment, he repaired to Strasbourg, Germany (1538-1541) to be pastor of a refugee congregation.

Here Calvin was successful in applying his principles of church order and ecclesiastical discipline that Geneva rejected. Here was a tiny yet powerful group of Reformed Christians that responded with joy and dedication to the concepts he felt were the cornerstone of church order: the election of lay members to offices of leadership and power.

The word "presbyter" (in Greek, presbyteros) was the name given to the elders who guided the life of the congregation, having been elected to this holy office by the people. In the New Testament, Presbyters were mentioned in the churches founded by St. Paul. The term seems to be used interchangeably with that of "bishop." In James 5:14 and I Peter 5:1 we have specific reference to their work and authority.

In the first centuries of the Christian Church, the word presbyter appears in the writings of I Clement, Ignatius, as well as in the Nicene Creed. Eventually the office of presbyter was absorbed into the priesthood to be recovered by the Biblical studies of Calvin and other Reformers.

Today, the Presbyterian and Reformed Churches follow a form of church government that is established on the concept of representative government—and from which all representative civil governments have taken as their model.

Congregations elect not only the elders to guide the destiny of each local church but presbyters to govern the affairs of groups of churches sharing the same doctrine and belief. These larger associations are called classes in the Reformed Church and Presbyteries in the Presbyterian Churches. The next higher judicatory is the synod, similar to the geographic size of a large state, and then the General Assembly, the national representative body.

All of this discussion of church government and order may seem like a weary exercise to some readers but to those steeped in the Reformation it was literally life or death. For the end of the old influence, power and discipline of Bishops and Popes left an enormous vacuum in the lives of people who chose to follow Luther and Calvin and the reformers. More than this, tension and conflict tore at the ranks of the new believers. Writes J. S. Whale:

No period was more critical for the Reformation than those years of 1530-1540 which saw Calvin's appearance on the stage of world history. It is arguable that he appeared just in time. For confusion and uncertainty were becoming widespread. The religious revolt against the medieval order, now nearly two decades old, seemed unable to move out of its first revolutionary phase, and to overcome its tendency to further division and disintegration. The individualism which its first leaders had let loose against the papal tradition of a thousand years was now recoiling upon itself.

All sorts of new religious groups sprang up. Some were sensitive but confused, having neither grounding in the New Testament nor the traditions of the Christian life. Others were rampant in their mystic dreams and wildly prophetic shouts of an end to the world. Society was churning and the church was turned upside down. Raw paganism took the place of sophisticated humanism. The lower classes stirred and the Peasants' Revolt of 1525 was put down in a bloody conflict with the Princes. It was a stark, shocking, exciting moment in history, and to this hour Calvin addressed his energies.

Many of these forces were breaking loose in Geneva and were probably the main inspiration of the call for Calvin's return from Strasbourg. He was a strong, determined man of iron. The city as well as the church required such a leader

in these turbulent days. Calvin returned and
before long, Geneva was to become the model
city of Europe and Presbyterianism the pattern
of Christian life wherever the Reformed Church
would plant itself: Switzerland, France, Holland,
Scotland, England, New England and all across
North America.

T. M. Lindsay of Scotland said that Calvin
did three things for Geneva—all of which extended far beyond the boundaries of the city.
"He gave its Church a trained ministry, its
homes an educated people who could give a
reason for their faith, and the whole city a heroic
soul which enabled the little town to stand forth
as the citadel and city of refuge for the op-
pressed Protestants of Europe."

For Calvin and Presbyterians then, the Church
of Christ existed where the Word of God is
preached, where the Sacraments (Baptism and
the Lord's Supper) are rightly administered and
received, but then Calvin added one more necessity—and where there is discipline. This
thoughtful, penetrating preacher, this scholar of
Bible and Word, would not yield to the threat
of mob rule nor the inherent pressures of kings
and princes. He was indeed, a Law and Order
leader—but the Law and Order essentially rose
from the ranks of the faithful and would not
be something imposed from above.

Communion, or the Lord's Supper, was as
central to Calvin's teaching as the centrality of
the pulpit and the exposition of the Word of
God through preaching. The fellowship of

Christians was that gathering of believers who
celebrated Holy Communion frequently and
faithfully. Fitness to come to the Lord's Table
was a key word in Calvin's vocabulary.

In the tradition of Calvin, one did not "join
the church" but was admitted to the Lord's
Table. This was both a right and duty of membership. To "sit at the table" was to share in
Holy Communion, formerly almost the absolute
right of the priesthood. Calvin now saw the
Christian experience as the "priesthood of all
believers." To continue in this fellowship meant
living a godly, upright and sober life. It was a
life of devotion and dedication. It was guarded
by discipline.

"It is certain," wrote Calvin in 1537, "that a
church cannot be called well-ordered and regulated unless in it the Holy Supper of our Lord
is often celebrated and attended—and this with
such good discipline that none dare present
himself at it save holily and with singular reverence." Calvin and his friends were dealing with
a raw and convulsive society. He meant what
he said. One could not be a serious follower
of Jesus Christ and also maintain crude habits
and violent ethics toward his neighbor. The result: Calvin and his elders were prepared, for
the sake of the Church, to judge the attitudes
and conduct of the flock. Should you step out
of line and shun suggestions for improved behavior and clean living, you could be excommu-
nicated. A surprising word for Protestants? Yes,
and Calvin added:

"For this reason, the discipline of excommunication, by which those may be corrected who are unwilling to govern themselves lovingly and by the Holy Word of God, is necessary in order to maintain the church in its integrity."

It is agreed that out of the Reformation were formed the two major branches of the Christian community: Lutheran and Reformed (Presbyterian). Luther held that in the Lord's Supper the body and blood of Christ are objectively present and actually partaken. The latter, in the tradition of Calvin, believe that these are "virtually present but spiritually partaken."

A lawyer by training but a theologian at heart, Calvin put much of his systematic writing into the *Institutes of the Christian Religion*. Out of this work came the order, system and authority that the new age of the sixteenth century was groping for. If the *Institutes* were the thoughts of Calvin, then Geneva was his workshop, for he implemented the convictions he held in pursuing the City of God among the world of man. Calvin was appreciative of the earlier work advanced by St. Augustine, especially when it came to a full definition of the Church.

Here Dr. Whale is helpful in our gaining the full impact of Calvin's thought and intention:

He begins by defining the Church as the whole company of the elect (a term related to an old Presbyterian favorite, pre-destination), not only men but angels, not only the living but also the dead; one society, one people of God; one Body, as it were, whose head is Christ, made up of those who in all ages and places since the beginning of the world have been called, united and sanctified according to the eternal providence of God. This invisible Church of the elect is one, universal and holy.

from *The Protestant Tradition.*

Theology is no easy science and Calvin's works are not of the same pace and content that we find in comic strips or the T.V. Guide. Yet any of us can catch a glimpse of the vast, soaring, and provocative teachings that came from the pen and preaching of this Reformer. For Calvin, man's aim in life was to know God and to glorify Him forever. The Bible was the ultimate source of such knowledge and the individual believer was given direction and insight through the power of the Holy Spirit.

In the turmoil and unrest of the sixteenth century, Calvin was firm and unyielding. When dealing with the famous heretic, Michael Servetus, Calvin did not flinch in pressing for the death penalty when Servetus refused to endorse the doctrine of the Trinity.

This event, in 1553, was a low point in the history of Geneva, normally a city of refuge and protection for dissenters, and certainly revealing a tyrannical side to Calvin's personality.

Servetus had been a Spanish scholar concerned about the souls of Moors and Jews. He felt that these diverse groups would have accepted Christianity if the Trinitarian doctrines were not required (i.e., that Father, Son and Holy Spirit were different essences of the same God). Because of his strong personal opinions and steady attack on orthodoxy, Servetus became the object of both Protestant and Catholic displeasure. He eventually was arrested in Geneva, sentenced, and burned at the stake.

Yet in Calvin's earlier writings, prior to the shocking episode which resulted in Servetus' death, were these words of concern and charity in dealing with non-Christians and non-believers:

> Far be it from us to approve as right those inhuman methods whereby many up to now have sought to force such people to accept our faith, denying them food, warmth and life's commonest amenities, and persecuting them with fire and sword.

Alas, Calvin could not sustain this benevolent mood when the case of Servetus presented itself. He was the prosecuting attorney that led to Servetus' death at the stake. Christians, both Catholic and Protestant have yielded to the acts of brutality, punishment, torture and death—all in the name of Christ. Unbridled zeal, and unchallenged authority can cause institutions as well as individuals to sin. It is at least gratifying to know that modern Calvinists, appalled at the gross acts committed in the sixteenth century, particularly the execution of Servetus, have

erected a monument in Geneva, with this in-
scription:

> Condemning an error which was that of his
> age, and firmly attached to liberty of con-
> science according to the true principles of
> the Reformation and the Gospel, we re-
> spectful sons of Calvin our great Reformer
> have erected this expiatory monument.

They knew he was wrong and they said it—a
quality of honesty that must be a part of every
Christian community.

Calvin's influence and example, his teaching
and persuasion were to be a fresh brook in
Geneva, a rushing stream in Scotland, and a
mighty river in America. Followers came to
Geneva to study and follow the Reformer. Not
surprisingly, France almost became Protestant,
then reverted to Catholicism. By 1560 there were
nearly two thousand Protestant Churches in
Calvin's homeland. Known as Huguenots (or
oath companions) they became a powerful un-
derground church, soon to surface and challenge
the Catholic establishment in politics as well as
religion. Open conflict ensued and the Massacre
of St. Bartholomew in Paris in 1572, saw the
sudden, shocking slaughter of nearly fifty thousand Huguenots. This blood-bath was followed
by intense persecution. During the next two
centuries, almost four million Protestants evac-
uated France, many of them migrating to Virginia and South Carolina.

In the Netherlands, both Calvin and Luther

had early followers, some tortured and imprisoned by the Spanish control. Eventually the influence of Calvin was to survive and become dominant. The Reformed Church in America, known popularly as the Dutch Reformed Church, traced its beginnings to the Netherlands. The first congregation was organized in 1628, in New Amsterdam, later to be called New York City. The Dutch West India Company had settled in 1625 and many of the first arrivals were of the Reformed persuasion. Eventually almost half of the population of Holland was to become attached to the Reformed faith. In America, the Dutch Protestants, like their Scottish Presbyterian counterparts, were to advance the cause of public education, the establishment of colleges and seminaries, and the insistence on a learned clergy.

As colonists settled the Hudson River Valley and pressed on into New Jersey, congregations were formed and the extension of Calvin and the Reformation spread far into the New World. Until the Revolution, the American Dutch Calvinists were subordinate to the classis (or synod) of the Reformed Church of Holland. Growth in the colonies extended swiftly after the Revolutionary War, reaching into the Middle West and on to the Far West.

By 1766, the leaders of the Dutch Reformed Church had been forceful in the shaping of Queen's College, now Rutgers University, with a charter that called for the "education of youth in the learned languages, liberal and useful arts and sciences, and especially in divinity, preparing them for the ministry and other good offices."

The zeal and dedication of the Dutch Protestants who followed Calvin was rarely equalled by any other national groups save the Scots. And here it was the fiery, determined, oft-persecuted John Knox who became a devoted follower of Calvin and in turn was to sway Scotland from Catholic rule to Presbyterian ascendency.

Scotland had nearly four centuries of Catholic control. Early dissenters like Patrick Hamilton, 1528, a disciple of Luther, and George Wishart, 1546, had been burned at the stake for their Protestant inclinations. Knox was no ordinary person. At one point he carried a saber to give Wishart protection. Noting this, Jasper Ridley in his outstanding biography of Knox, observed,

> There is something symbolic in the first appearance on the page of history of the leading figures of the Reformation. Calvin first appears at his writing-desk, already writing a learned tome at the age of twenty-three. Cranmer is first seen burrowing in the Bible to find scriptural texts to justify his king in divorcing his wife and marrying his mistress. Luther's first appearance was more vigorous, nailing his theses to the door of the church in Wittenberg, striking at the old Church with every blow of the hammer. But Knox is the only one who enters carrying a two-handed sword. . . . It was through armed organization that Knox was to fulfill his mission.

But not before he would see the martyrdom of Wishart, his own imprisonment and sentence to eighteen months as a French galley slave. Not before he would make his way to Geneva, be tutored and inspired by Calvin and then return to become the catalyst of Scottish independence, politics and religious freedom in the affairs of Faith.

By 1560, Knox had fired the Scottish nation to storm against Catholic control, bringing down churches and monasteries that formally symbolized the rule of Rome and the powerful Mary, Queen of Scots. In that year the Scottish Parliament abolished Catholicism and replaced it with the Protestant forms advocated by Knox, furnishing a constitution and confession that was intensely Calvinistic. For many years Knox controlled Scotland from his pulpit in Edinburgh. He was a determined, hard, often ruthless pursuer of the Faith—as he saw it. One of his victims was Mary Queen of Scots.

The Calvin-Knox notions of free public education and representative government were to flourish in Scotland and expand into the New World. Much groundwork was laid for the theological support of the Revolution of 1776. For at the heart of the Presbyterian teaching was the conviction that the individual believer, when forced to make the choice of being loyal to God or yielding to a Prince or King, must choose to serve God. When this doctrine became broadly supported, it really meant the end of the Divine Right of Kings and the formation of true democracy within Church and State. Shouted Knox:

Now the common song of all men is: We
must obey our kings, be they good or be
they bad; for God hath so commanded. But
horrible shall the vengeance be that shall
be poured forth upon such blasphemers of
God's holy name and ordinance. For it is
no less blasphemy to say that God hath
commanded kings to be obeyed when they
command impiety, than to say that God by
His precept is author and maintainer of all
iniquity. True it is, God hath commanded
kings to be obeyed, but like true it is, that
in things which they commit against His
glory, or when cruelly without cause they
rage against their brethren, the members of
Christ's body, He hath commanded no obedience, but rather He hath approved, yea,
and greatly rewarded such as have opposed
themselves to their ungodly commandments and blind rage.

The flow of Presbyterians into the New World
was substantial. Both Scotland and the Netherlands were to supply much of the leadership
for North American settlements which cherished
the freedom of religion and sought to implement
the teachings of Christ into daily life. For Presbyterians, political freedom and religious
independence were inseparable. It is not surprising that Presbyterian clergyman John With-
erspoon should be a signer of the Declaration
of Independence (and the only minister so
listed). The English made no bones about it

when they said that the American Revolution
was a Presbyterian Rebellion.

Major denominations now fulfilling the Presbyterian and Reformed heritage today are the
United Presbyterian Church, the Reformed
Church in America, the Presbyterian Church in
the United States, Christian Reformed Church,
and the Evangelical and Reformed Church
which merged with the General Council of the
Congregational Christian Churches to form the
United Church of Christ in 1957.

Influential groups of Presbyterian descent are
located in almost every country today. In Hol-
land, Switzerland and France, members of the
Reformed Church are everywhere to be found.
Presbyterians are now the majority group in
Scotland.

The Wisdom of
JOHN CALVIN

TRUE AND SUBSTANTIAL wisdom principally consists of two parts, the knowledge of God and the knowledge of ourselves. No man can take a survey of himself but must immediately turn to the contemplation of God, in whom he "lives and moves."

It is plain that no man can arrive at the true knowledge of himself, without having first contemplated the divine character, and then descended to the consideration of his own. For, such is the native pride of us all, we invariably esteem ourselves righteous, innocent, wise and holy, till we are convinced by clear proofs, of our unrighteousness, turpitude, folly and impurity. But we are never thus convinced, while we confine our attention to ourselves, and regard not the Lord, who is the only standard by which this judgment ought to be formed.

If at noonday we look either on the ground or at any surrounding objects, we conclude our vision to be very strong and piercing; but when we raise our eyes and steadily look at the sun, they are at once dazzled and confounded with such a blaze of brightness, and we are constrained to confess that our sight, so piercing in viewing terrestrial things, when directed to the sun, is dimness itself.

The nature of pure and genuine religion consists of faith, united with a serious fear of God, comprehending a voluntary reverence, and producing legitimate worship agreeable to the injunctions of the law . . . while great ostentation in ceremonies is universally displayed, but sincerity of heart is rarely to be found.

The worship of God . . . is the only thing which renders men superior to brutes, and makes them aspire to immortality.

While experience testifies that the seeds of religion are sown by God in every heart, we scarcely find one man in a hundred who cherishes what he has received, and not one in whom they grow to maturity, much less bear fruit in due season.

Withersoever you turn your eyes, there is not an atom of the world in which you cannot behold some brilliant sparks at least of his glory.

For, as persons who are old, or whose eyes are by any means become dim, if you show them the most beautiful book, though they perceive something written, but can scarcely read two words together, yet by the assistance of spectacles, will begin to read distinctly—so the Scripture, collecting in our minds the otherwise confused notions of Diety, dispels the darkness, and gives us a clear view of the true God.

The Scripture will be only effectual to produce the saving knowledge of God, when the certainty of it shall be founded on the internal persuasion of the Holy Spirit.

Persons who, abandoning the Scripture, imagine to themselves some other way of approaching God, must be considered as not so much misled by error as actuated by frenzy.

It is incumbent on us diligently to read and attend to the Scripture, if we would receive any advantage or satisfaction from the Spirit of God. He is the author of Scriptures; he cannot be mutable and inconsistent with himself.

We maintain that the essence of the one God, which pertains to the Father, to the Son, and to the Spirit, is simple and undivided, and on the other hand, that the Father is, by some property distinguished from the Son, and likewise the Son from the Spirit. . . . I trust that the whole substance of this doctrine has been faithfully stated and explained, provided my readers set bounds to their curiosity, and are not unreasonably fond of tedious and intricate controversies.

Whenever we call God the Creator of heaven and earth, let us at the same time reflect . . . that we are his children, whom he has received into his charge and custody, to be supported and educated; so that we may expect every blessing from him alone, and cherish certain hope that he will never suffer us to want those things which are necessary to our well-being, that our hope may depend on no other; that, whatever we need or desire, our prayers may be directed to him, and that, from whatever quarter we receive any advantage, we may acknowledge it to be his benefit, and confess it with thanksgiving.

The beginning of our recovery and salvation is the restoration which we obtain through Christ. . . . This is the end of regeneration, that Christ may form us anew in the image of God.

He who has fixed the limits of our life, has also intrusted us with the care of it; has furnished us with means and supplies for its preservation; has also made us provident of dangers; and that they may not oppress us unawares, has furnished us with cautions and remedies.

The arts of deliberation and caution in men proceed from the inspiration of God.

Original sin appears to be an hereditary depravity and corruption of our nature, diffused through all the parts of the soul, rendering us obnoxious to the Divine wrath, and producing in us those works which the Scripture calls "works of the flesh."

All men are overwhelmed with an inevitable calamity, from which they can never emerge unless they are extricated by the mercy of God.

As by the precepts God disturbs the consciences of the impious, that they may not enjoy too much pleasure in sin without any recollection of his judgments.

What could be more vain or frivolous than for men to offer the fetid stench arising from the fat of cattle, in order to reconcile themselves to God? or to resort to any aspersion of water or of blood, to cleanse themselves from pollution? In short, the whole legal worship, if it be considered in itself, and contain no shadows and figures of correspondent truths, will appear perfectly ridiculous.

All ceremonies of the law are worthless and vain.

In the precepts of the law, God appears only, on the one hand, as the rewarder of perfect righteousness, of which we are all destitute; and on the other, as the severe judge of transgressions. But in Christ, his face shines with a plenitude of grace and lenity, even towards miserable and unworthy sinners.

"Thou shalt not kill"—the common sense of mankind will perceive nothing more than that we ought to abstain from all acts of injury to others, and from all desire to commit any such acts. I maintain that it implies that we should do every thing that we possibly can towards the preservation of the life of our neighbor.

The Lord's Day—the principal thing to be remembered is the general doctrine; that lest religion decay or languish among us, sacred assemblies ought diligently to be held, and that we ought to use those external means which are adapted to support the worship of God.

Every man ought to consider himself as charged with the safety of all.

The conjugal union [of marriage] is appointed as a remedy for our necessity, that we may not break out into unrestrained licentiousness.

Let juniors revere old age, since the Lord has designed that age to be honorable.

Let old men, by their prudence and superior experience, guide the imbecility of youth; not teasing them with sharp and clamorous invectives, but tempering severity with mildness and affability.

His is the best and most holy life, who lives as little as possible to himself, and no man leads a worse or more iniquitous life, than he who lives exclusively to himself, and makes his own interest the sole object of his thoughts and pursuits.

Christ has received of the Father power to forgive sins, to raise up whom he will, to bestow righteousness, holiness and salvation; that he is appointed to be Judge of the living and the dead, that he may receive the same honor as the Father.

Therefore, that faith may find in Christ a solid ground of salvation, the office that was assigned to him by the Father consists of three parts: Prophet, King and Priest.

Since we see that the whole of our salvation is comprehended in Christ, we must be cautious not to alienate from him the least possible portion of it. If we seek salvation, we are taught by the name of JESUS, that it is in him; if we seek any other gifts of the Spirit, they will be found in his unction; strength, in his dominion; purity, in his conception; indulgence discovers itself in his nativity, by which he was made to resemble us in all things, that he might learn to condole with us; if we seek redemption, it will be found in his passion; absolution, in his condemnation; remission of the curse, in his cross; satisfaction, in his sacrifice; purification, in his blood; reconciliation, in his descent into hell; mortification of the flesh, in his sepulchre;

newness of life and immortality, in his resurrection; the inheritance of celestial kingdom, in his entrance into heaven; protection, security, abundance and enjoyment of all blessings, in his kingdom; a fearless expectation of the judgment, in the judicial authority committed to him. Finally, blessings of every kind are deposited in him; let us draw from his treasury, and from no other source, till our desires are satisfied.

True piety consists rather in a pure and true zeal which loves God altogether as Father, and reveres him truly as Lord, embraces his justice and dreads to offend him more than to die. All those who possess this zeal do not undertake to forge for themselves a God as their temerity wishes, but they seek the knowledge of the true God from that very God and do not conceive him otherwise than he manifests and declares himself to them.

From God's word . . . we learn that our only eternal God is the spring and fountain of all life, justice, wisdom, virtue, goodness and clemency.

At first man was formed in the image and resemblance of God in order that man might admire his Author in the adornments with which he had been nobly vested by God, and honor him with proper acknowledgment. But having trusted such a great excellence of his nature and having forgotten from whom it had come and by whom it subsisted, man strove to raise himself up apart from the Lord. Hence man had to be stripped of all God's gifts of which he was foolishly proud, so that, denuded and deprived of all glory, he might know God whom man, after having been enriched by his liberalities, had dared to despise.

For, though we are composed of a soul and a body, yet we feel nothing but the flesh.

Hence there is no doubt that faith is a light of the Holy Spirit through which our understandings are enlightened and our hearts are confirmed in a sure persuasion which is assured that the truth of God is so certain that he can but accomplish that which he has promised through his holy word that he will do.

For he [Christ] has put on our flesh in order that, being made Son of man, he would make us children of God together with himself; and having received on himself our poverty, he would transfer his riches to us; having taken on himself our weakness, he would confirm us by his power; having accepted our mortality, he would give us his immortality; and being descended to earth, he would raise us to heaven.

The Church is . . . set forth to us as object of faith to this end that we may have confidence that all the elect are conjoined through the bond of faith in one Church and society, in one people of God, of which Christ our Lord is the leader and prince and head.

Hope is nothing else than the expectation of the things that faith has believed to be truly promised by God.

Prayer is similar to a communication between God and us whereby we expose to him our desires, our joys, our sighs, in a word, all the thoughts of our hearts.

Baptism serves likewise as our acknowledgment of faith in the sight of men; because it is a mark by which we publicly declare that we wish to be numbered among the people of God, to the end that we, together with all believers, may serve and honor, with one same religion, one God.

[The Supper of the Lord] confirms to us that the body of the Lord has once for all been given in such a way for us, that it is now ours and will be ours perpetually. It confirms that his blood has once been shed in such a way for us that it will be always ours.

Now, this discipline [excommunication] is necessary among believers because, as the Church is the body of Christ, she must not be polluted and contaminated by such stinking and rotten members who dishonor the head; moreover, in order that the saints be not (as it is usual to happen) corrupted and spoiled by the company of the bad.

For the Lord affirms that the fact that kings rule, that counselors order just things and that the great of the earth are judges, is a work of his wisdom. . . . On the other hand, the mutual duty of subjects and citizens is not only to honor and to revere their superiors, but to recommend by prayers to the Lord their salvation and prosperity, to submit willingly to their rule, to obey their laws and constitutions, and not to refuse the chores imposed by them: be they taxes, tolls, tributes and other contributions, or be they offices, civic commissions and all the like. . . . But from obedience to superiors we must always accept one thing: that it does not draw us away from obedience to Him to whose edicts the commands of all kings must yield.

But as the bare history would not be enough, and . . . would be of no advantage for salvation, the Evangelists do not merely relate that Christ was born, and that he died and vanquished death, but also explain for what purpose he was born, and died, and rose again, and what benefit we derive from those events.

We must also remember the ambiguous signification of the word faith; for frequently faith signifies the sound doctrine of piety. . . . On the contrary, it is sometimes restricted to a particular object . . . and we have lately shown, that Paul uses faith for the gift of miracles; which is possessed by those who are neither

regenerated by the Spirit of God, nor serious
worshippers of him. In another place, also, he
uses it to denote the instruction by which we
are edified in the faith.

Not one of the prophets opened his mouth
. . . without having first received the words from
the Lord. . . . What could proceed from the
pollution of the one, and the folly of the other,
but impure and foolish speeches, if they had
spoken their own words?

Till our minds are fixed on the Spirit, Christ
remains of no value to us; because we look at
him as an object of cold speculation without
us, and therefore at a great distance from us.

He ascribes to [the Holy Spirit] the peculiar
office of suggesting to their minds all the oral
instructions which he had given them. For in
vain would the light present itself to the blind,
unless this Spirit of understanding would open
their mental eyes; so that he may be justly called
the key with which the treasures of the kingdom
of heaven are unlocked to us; and his illumination constitutes our mental eyes to behold
them.

For the Scripture is the true touchstone
whereby all doctrines must be tried. If any man
say that this kind of trial is doubtful, forasmuch
as the Scripture is oftentimes doubtful, and is
interpreted divers ways, I say, that we must also

add the judgment of the Spirit, who is, not without cause, called the Spirit of discretion. But the faithful must judge of every doctrine not otherwise than out of and according to the Scriptures, having the Spirit for their leader and guide.

We must remember, that the Scripture is not only given us, but that interpreters and teachers are also added, to be helps to us.

We are certain, as long as we continue in the bosom of the Church, that we shall remain in possession of the truth.

Whoever then desires to be deemed a servant of God, and a teacher in his Church . . . must be endued with the Spirit of God.

They who answer, that the word of God is the rule by which everything that men bring forward ought to be tried, say something, but not the whole. I grant that doctrines ought to be tested by God's word; but except the Spirit of wisdom be present, to have God's word in our hands will avail little or nothing, for its meaning will not appear to us.

Many are immediately satisfied with but moderate information, and as soon as they understand a portion of any subject, they reject every addition, and many too often settle down at the first elements, and their obstinacy prevents that complete knowledge which is necessary.

God, we know, is subject to no passions; and we know that no change takes place in him.

Moses . . . declares that the Lord had undertaken the labour of making garments of skins for Adam and his wife. It is not indeed proper so to understand his words, as if God had been a furrier, or a servant to sew clothes. Now, it is not credible that skins should have been presented to them by chance; but, since animals had before been destined for their use, being now impelled by a new necessity, they put some to death, in order to cover themselves with their skins, having been divinely directed to adopt this counsel; therefore Moses calls God the Author of it.

In us there is no affection unaccompanied by sin, because they all exceed due bounds and proper restraint; but when Christ was distressed by grief and fear, he did not rise against God, but continued to be regulated by the true rule of moderation.

If the love of ourselves hinders us from following Christ, we must resist it courageously.

While Christ forgives the sins of men, he does not overturn political order, or reverse the sentences and punishments.

The knowledge of faith consists more in certainty than in comprehension.

When we inculcate that faith ought to be certain and secure, we conceive not a certainty attended with no doubt, or a security interrupted by no anxiety; but we rather affirm, that believers have a perpetual conflict with their own diffidence, and are far from placing their consciences in a placid calm, never disturbed by any storms.

The pious heart therefore perceives a division in itself, being partly affected with delight, through a knowledge of the Divine goodness; partly distressed with sorrow, through a sense of its own calamity; partly relying on the promise of the gospel; partly trembling at the evidence of its own iniquity; partly exulting in the apprehension of life; partly alarmed by the fear of death.

How weak soever we may then be, yet our salvation is not uncertain, because it is sustained by God's power. Hence is its security, not only for the present, but also for the future.

For obedience is the source, not only of an absolutely perfect and complete faith, but of all right knowledge of God.

. . . since I was too obstinately devoted to the superstitions of the Popery to be easily extricated from so profound an abyss of mire, God by a sudden conversion subdued and brought my mind to a teachable frame which was more hardened in such matters than might have been expected from one at my early period of life.

To separate faith from trust would be equal to the attempt to separate heat and light from the sun.

It must be remembered that every word which may have issued forth from God is to be received with implicit authority.

Our wisdom ought to consist in embracing with gentle docility and without exception, all that is delivered in the sacred Scriptures.

We see that all are placed under the same regulation, in order that they may submit themselves with gentleness and docility of mind to be governed by the pastors who are appointed for this purpose.

Faith is properly that by which we obey the gospel.

Caesar without the republic is not Caesar, the republic without Caesar is not the republic.

God, by a sudden conversion tamed and made teachable my mind.

[Calvin] was so obstinately addicted to the papal superstition that it was by no means easy to extricate himself from this quagmire.

For when I descended into myself or raised my heart to Thee, such a sense of horror gripped me that no purifications, no satisfactions could assuage. And the more I examined myself, the sharper became the stings of conscience, so much so that there remained for me not other solace or comfort but to deceive myself in forgetfulness. But as nothing better offered I went on in the same train as I had commenced until there supervened a very different form of doctrine, not for the purpose of turning us away from the Christian profession, but to bring it back to its true source and restore it, purified from all filth, in its purity.

Having thus been imbued with some taste of true piety I was straightway inflamed with so great a desire to profit from it that, although I did not altogether quit my other studies, I gave myself to them more slackly. Now I was completely astonished that, before a year passed, all those who had some desire for pure doctrine gathered themselves about me in order to learn, although I had made but a beginning myself.

We know by experience that singing is fitted powerfully to move and inflame the hearts of men as a means of invoking and praising God with a more vehement and ardent zeal.

Such great things has the advent of Jesus Christ operated that everything is changed. There is a new heaven and a new earth. He enables us to ascend into heaven. Heaven is opened and by His own revealed Word God has disclosed Himself to us. We have entered the portals of God and see those things which are hid in Him.

Wonderful is the sacrament which joins God to man, and also man to God, so that in a marvellous fashion God appropriated the body of Christ to Himself that it might be a peculiar tabernacle of His own habitation.

After having long tried to find out what a heretic is, I can discover no other answer than that we esteem all those heretics who do not agree with us in our opinions.

The ancient Church established patriarchates and set primates over separate provinces in order, by this means, the better to bind the bishops in concord. In the same manner it is right that today one archbishop should preside over the illustrious kingdom of Poland, not indeed that he should dominate others or arrogate to himself an authority filched from them, but that for the sake of order he should hold the first place in synods and nurture a holy unity among his colleagues. Similarly there might be bishops of cities and provinces for the purpose of preserving order, as circumstances require, and one elected by his colleagues should be charged with this duty on the occasion of episcopal assemblies. But it is a very different thing to confer on a man a moderate dignity of this kind, in accordance with the powers which it involves, from investing in one man an immense dominion over the whole earth. Entirely worthless, therefore, is the chatter of the Romanists about one supreme head. It is in accordance neither with the sacred ordinance of God nor with the sacred usage of the ancient Church.

God is not known where there is no religion, no piety, which consists in faith joined with a living fear of God.

The Word is the instrument by which the Lord dispenses to believers the illumination of His Spirit.

If the authority of the ancient Church has any weight among us, let us observe that, for the space of five hundred years or thereabout, during the period when Christianity was in its greatest vigour and there was the greatest purity of doctrine, the Christian Churches were in common clean and exempt from such pollution.

Human reason can never approach or address itself to the truth in understanding what is the true God and what is His will towards us.

Nevertheless, in order that no one may esteem man to be very happy in that we concede to him so great a virtue in comprehending things inferior appertaining to this corruptible world, it is necessary to bear in mind that this faculty of understanding, which he possesses, and the intelligence which results from it, is a fleeting thing and of no importance before God, when there is no firm foundation of truth to rest on.

From the first movement even until the last perseverance the good we do is of God in all its parts.

Faith consists in the knowledge of God and of Christ, not in reverence for the Church.

The end of the struggle is always such that faith surmounts these difficulties by which it is besieged, and which seem to imperil it.

Revolt from the church is denial of God and Christ.

We do not deny that the churches which Antichrist [the Pope] dominates by his tyranny remain churches. But we say that he has profaned them by his sacrilegious impiety, that he has afflicted them by his inhuman domination, that he has poisoned them with false and wicked doctrines, and that he has corrupted and, as it were, put them to death, so much that Jesus Christ is half buried, the Gospel strangled,

Christianity exterminated, the service of God almost abolished. In short, all is so disfigured that there appears rather an image of Babylon than of the holy city of God.

If we look in the face of the system of ecclesiastical government which is in vogue today throughout the whole papacy, we shall find no such excessive brigandage the world over. Assuredly the whole thing is so different from and so repugnant to the institution of Christ, and so remote from the ancient form, so contradictory to both nature and reason, that one could not do a greater injury to Christ than to claim His name as a colour for such a disordered and depraved regime.

. . . since God has faithfully comprised in His Word and has fully declared what is the whole true rule of justice, the whole manner of worshipping Him aright, and all that is necessary for our salvation, it is incumbent on us to hear Him as our sole master in these things. As to external order and ceremonies, He has not willed to ordain in particular and, as it were, word by word what we are to observe, since He foresaw that this depends on the diversity of the times, and that one form would not be proper and useful for every age. Therefore we must have recourse to those general rules which He has given, so that whatever the necessity of the Church may demand for the observance of order and decency may be considered in accordance with them.

[A sacrament] is an external sign, by which God seals in our consciences the promises of His goodwill towards us in order to sustain the weakness of our faith, whereby we mutually render testimony to our piety before Him and the angels as well as men.

Civil government is, therefore, a vocation, not only holy and legitimate before God, but also the most sacred and honourable among all others.

When I first came here [Geneva] there was almost no organization. The gospel was preached and that was all. Everything was in upheaval. I have lived through many marvellous conflicts. I have been greeted in mockery in the evening before my own door with fifty or sixty shots. You may imagine how this affected a poor, timid scholar such as I am and, I confess, always have been. Then I was hunted out of the town, and on my return from Strasbourg, I had as great difficulty as before in performing my office. People set their dogs on me, which caught at my robe and my legs. . . . When I went to the Council of Two Hundred to appease a tumult, I was greeted with cries to withdraw. "I shall do nothing of the sort. Kill me, you rascals, if you will. My blood will witness against you, and these benches will require it of you." So it will be with you, my brethren, for you are in the midst of a perverse and unhappy people. However many persons of goodwill there be, it is a wicked and perverse folk, and you will have experience of its perversity when I am gone. But take courage and fortify yourselves; for God will make use of this Church and maintain and preserve it. I have had many failings with which you have had to put up, and all I have done is worth nothing. The wicked will lay hold of this saying. But I repeat that all I have done is of no worth, and that I am a miserable creature. This, however, I can say . . . I have wished to do good and my failings have always displeased me, and the fear of God has been rooted in my heart. So that you can say that my intention has been good, and I pray that the evil may be pardoned me, and if there has been anything good, that you will conform to it and follow it.

Concerning my doctrine, I have taught faithfully and God has given me the grace to write. I have done this as faithfully as possible and have not corrupted a single passage of Scripture, nor knowingly twisted it. When I have been tempted to subtlety, I have withstood the temptation and always studied simplicity. I have never written anything from hatred of anyone, but have always faithfully set before me what I deemed to be the glory of God.

JOHN WESLEY

About
JOHN WESLEY

"NOT A NEW religion, but the old religion of the Bible . . . of the primitive church . . . of the Church of England . . . no other than the love of God to all mankind."

With those words John Wesley laid the cornerstone of the Chapel named after him in 1777, in Moorfields, London and gave expression to his belief on the meaning and purpose of Methodism. Never did he expect to be the founder of a "new religion" nor the cause for the separation of thousands of believers into another denomination of Christianity. He was reaching for a deeper faith, a stronger, more constant flow of faith into works. His life was filled with the one major quest: to be a true follower of Jesus Christ. As he moved toward that goal, he was to draw countless men and women into the sphere of his influence and persuasion. Out of this would come the Methodist Church, one of the largest branches of Protestant Christianity and certainly one shaped dramatically by the force and energy of a single solitary Englishman.

Wesley was born in the Rectory of Epworth,

a small community some hundred miles north of London, on June 28, 1703. His father, the Reverend Samuel Wesley was a curate of several Church of England parishes before serving, with his wife, Susanna, for thirty-eight years in Epworth. This rugged and devout couple had nineteen children and somehow managed to raise them on the annual salary of sixty pounds (about one hundred and fifty dollars) a year.

Sickness, disease, and unending debt seemed to be the regular diet for this eighteenth century household. For young John, childhood was to be as thrilling and dangerous as the encounters and journeys of later years.

When Wesley was six, a group of Epworth malcontents set fire to the thatch roof of the Rectory while the family was asleep. Sparks and smoke quickly spread through the entire house. An alert maid rounded up most of the children, carrying one baby and leading the rest to safety—all but John. The wind sucked flames up the staircase and his father found he could not reach his son on the upper level.

Now the roof was nearly gone, the entire staircase a wall of flame. Suddenly the lad appeared at the second story window. There were no ladders or ropes available, so a small man jumped up on the shoulders of a tall bystander and lowered the boy to safety. In his Journal, Wesley was to recall every detail of the harrowing night:

I saw streaks of fire on the top of my room.

I got up and ran to the door, but I could get no further, all the floor beyond it being ablaze. I then climbed upon a chest which stood near the window.

For the rest of his life John Wesley was to believe that he was spared by God for some special purpose. Time and again, in storms at sea, facing mobs and threats, struggling with sickness or sorrow, he felt that the providence of God was about him until his work was complete.

If John Wesley is considered the Father of Methodism, then Susanna Wesley is the Mother. From her devotion to the Christian life, her determination that her household should be committed believers, and the unceasing desire to glorify God in all that was said and done marked her world view. Centuries before Women's Liberation, Susanna was an informal lay leader, reading the scriptures, leading the prayers and "other persuasions" of local townsmen that stopped at the Epworth manse. Her husband, true to the Church of England's rigidity of mind and practice, questioned her activity and challenged her behavior. During one absence, she replied to his critical letters by saying,

I cannot conceive why any should reflect upon you because your wife endeavours to draw people to church, and to restrain them from profaning the Lord's Day, by reading to them and other persuasions. For my part I value no censure upon this ac-

count. . . . As to looking particular, I grant
it does. And so does almost anything that
is serious, or that may any way advance
the glory of God or the salvation of souls.

And she was vitally concerned about salvation,
the saving of her own household and the proclamation of the life of Jesus Christ to all who
would listen. This force of care and urgency was
to mark the lives of John and his brother,
Charles, who would share in the formation and
growth of the Methodist Church. But not before
long years of searching, disappointment and
travel.

Young Wesley attended Charterhouse School,
went on to Oxford University where he became
a scholar, and was later recognized as a Fellow
of Lincoln College in 1726. Following ordination
in the Church of England he was to continue
as a distinguished Bible student, also recognized
for his grasp of organizational affairs. While his
brother Charles attended Oxford, John assisted
his father in parish duties at Epworth. Charles
was immediately successful in gathering a small
group of students intent on building a firm faith,
sharing in prayer and worship, and pursuing all
this with regularity and diligence. Others who
did not share their fervor but observed their
schedule referred to them, in derisive tones, as
Methodists.

Charles was personally responsible for this
Evangelical Revival. A "Holy Club" was formed
and the student members vowed to attend regu-

lar Bible sessions, attend Holy Communion at least once a week, and specific forms of Christian service. John returned to Oxford in 1729 and quickly became the new leader of this student Christian enterprise. Out of this group was to come George Whitfield, one of the primary leaders of the Methodist Church and noted throughout the country for his powerful, persuasive preaching.

At this point a brief explanation about religious organization during the eighteenth century might be in order. The Wesleys were all members of the Church of England—as were most of the citizens of their day. Christianity officially came to Britain with St. Augustine's mission to Canterbury in A.D. 597. As early as the second century, missionaries had appeared in Ireland, Scotland and the islands of Iona.

Loyalty, discipline, and direction of the Christian community came from the Pope in Rome, as it did in varying degrees throughout the countries of Western Europe.

As the Roman Empire began to lose its grip and influence in national life, strong rulers and kings emerged to express control in matters of the Church as well as the State. Nationalism became a serious problem for the Vatican since it had in history been so closely identified with the Holy Roman Empire. The historic British document, the Magna Carta has one phrase that states dramatically, "The Church of England shall be free." In 1215, there was a move to have a greater local participation in the election of

Bishops. Thus a three way struggle continued to exist between the Pope, the King and the local religious bodies.

Although challenged, the Pope's control and influence in Great Britain lasted until Henry VIII. Around 1531-1535 Henry successfully forced a complete break with Rome, persuading Parliament and the English clergy to repudiate papal authority and make him head of Church and State. Our readers who have seen "Anne of a Thousand Days" and "A Man for All Seasons" will recall the tension, drama and excitement of these years.

The result was the Church of England, which continued to be Episcopal in government (meaning ruled by bishops; the Greek word, episkopos, means overseer) retained much of the Roman Catholic form of worship, holy orders and church architecture. The Book of Common Prayer, adapted from medieval Latin sources was translated into the English language by Thomas Cranmer, Archbishop of Canterbury. Favored by Henry VIII, he also saw to it that the Bible was also available to the English reader. During this same time in history, Martin Luther and John Calvin were separating large groups from Catholic control in Germany, France and Switzerland. This time of Reformation had different results in every country. Two hundred years later, with the appearance of John Wesley, we find the Church of England to have become loaded with regulations, forms and apathy.

With this background—a Church that seemed to lack Christian vitality and seemed quite distant from the fire and enthusiasm of the reports given in the New Testament account of religious fellowship—Wesley turned to a course of prayer, Bible reading and discussion as a means to revive his own faith and that of his friends.

Right at this moment in his personal religious development a book was published by William Law, *Serious Call to a Devout and Holy Life*. The author urged the application of faith to life in a most practical way. Outward rules and form were replaced by inward discipline and strong measures of personal piety . . . such as getting up at 5 a.m. for private devotion (reading of scripture and prayer).

The opening lines of Law's book seemed to be written directly at John Wesley:

Devotion signifies a life given or devoted to God.

And this devotion to God was clearly shown in the illustrations provided by Law—the mother at home, the merchant and businessman, the minister in a country parish—all were filled with a sense of purpose and a personality surrounded with happiness.

Wesley was inclined to this strategy of Christian perfection. Not that he wanted to be holier than others or recognized as a saint among sinners. Far from that. His desire was to be a better person, a more faithful Christian and Law's plea that, "if we are to follow Christ, it must be in our common way of spending every day." This meant, among other things, a carefully, even rigidly planned hourly schedule. Get up early. Pursue private devotions for at least an hour. Have fellowship of prayer, Bible reading and Christian conversation with members of the household. Law went further to state that he did not feel he should have his own breakfast until some act of charity, every day, be done to aid the poor, lonely or aged. Often Law would milk a cow before breakfast and deliver the milk to the poor within his community. The Christian life was a daily experience of love and concern directed to others and a steady maintenance of self-discipline and striving for solid spiritual growth.

Law, next to Susanna Wesley, had the most telling impact on John Wesley and his brother and friends of the Holy Club. They accepted not only the rules of personal piety and worship, but plunged into the acts of charity so essential to the practical application of the Gospel.

Their early strikes into the heartland of human woe and misery were to become the hallmark of Methodism and the gathering rise of membership and following. Hardly half a dozen, the Holy Club regularly visited the sick and deprived, taking them food and the comfort of conversation and prayer. Some of the poor and destitute were taught to read and were given the Scriptures. Visits were made to the prisons, as well as to the families of prisoners. The young men gave money from their own slender incomes and regularly begged for funds from friends and strangers.

John Wesley then followed these activities with a brief and uneasy assignment in the new colony of Georgia, under the invitation of General Oglethorpe, Governor appointed by the Crown. Wesley was particularly interested in bringing the Gospel to the American Indians. Yet neither the influential Oglethorpe, nor the American frontier had as much long range impact upon Wesley as his encounter with some shipboard companions seeking the freedom of the New World. These were Moravians, a much persecuted religious sect from Eastern Europe. Their simple devotion and absolute faith were finally the factors to spring Wesley into a totally new religious dimension—a conversion to Jesus Christ and a personal experience of salvation.

For those raised within the traditions of the Church, familiar with the Creed, educated to the contents of the Holy Bible, skilled in the organization of religious societies, it seems strange to speak of their conversion to Jesus Christ. Yet it was John Wesley's claim that he had known all the information of Faith but never had really experienced the power of the Holy Spirit. It came to him on May 24, 1738 in London, following his return from a disappointing stay in America.

In the evening I went very unwillingly to a Society in Aldersgate Street, where one was reading Luther's 'Preface to the Epistle of Romans'. About a quarter before nine, while he was describing the change which God works in the heart through faith in Christ, I felt my heart strangely warmed. I felt I did trust in Christ, Christ alone for my salvation; and an assurance was given me that He had taken away my sins, even mine, and saved me from the law of sin and death.

From this lasting experience, John Wesley became the most famous itinerant preacher in the world. Since the masses were not to be found in the established churches (and he was frequently barred from speaking there anyway) Wesley went where they would naturally gather—out of doors. Preaching services were held in town squares, along the docks and wharfs, near factories, out in open fields. It was not unusual in the later years of Wesley's fame, for him to address twenty thousand people on a hillside.

Charles Wesley was known as the poet of the Methodist movement. Hymn and song writer, he composed some of the most popular music now in the collection of the Christian Church. John did not anticipate the founding of a new church. He called his local groups societies and they were established almost wherever and whenever he preached. And how regularly and widely he preached! It is estimated that he travelled on horseback more than five thousand miles a year.

Wesley turned his organizing skill to the mass-following that grew. He trained laymen in preaching and Biblical exposition, sending them on regular "circuits" to sustain the new members and encourage their growth in the Christian life. The first Methodist Conference was called in 1744, where several Methodist ministers joined with John in this official act. Wesley, in spite of the rebuff of the Church of England, remained loyal to his ordination. Yet the American revolution put new pressures on his relationship with the Church of England which was committed to the Tory cause and the position of George III. Wesley resolved this dilemma by ordaining two missionaries sent to America, giving them the power to administer the sacraments—Baptism and the Lord's Supper.

The Rev. Dr. Thomas Coke was also ordained as Superintendent and in turn, in the Colonies, ordained Francis Asbury, later known as Bishop Asbury and probably the most important Methodist figure in the life of the new nation.

American Methodists consider the Christmas conference of 1784 to be the time of origin for the branch in the U.S. The form of church government followed was mainly Episcopalian, but emphasis was placed on its utility rather than on the idea of the bishop being in the line of apostolic succession. Conferences on the district, regional and national level govern the affairs of the church. Laymen are represented in this structure. Bishops are elected by the Jurisdictional and Central Conferences and meet at least once a year.

Methodists have their largest following in the United States, with more than 10 million members. Worldwide the followers of Wesley are found in more than 50 nations, showing particular strength in Australia. Methodists are active participants in the ecumenical movement of the Christian community, support extensive programs of outreach through radio and television. Their publishing concerns are some of the largest in the world. Presently more than 100 colleges and universities in the United States alone trace their origin to the Methodist Church.

The Wisdom of JOHN WESLEY

IN SOME OF THE following days I snatched a few hours, to read *The History of the Puritans*. I stand in amaze. First, at the execrable spirit of persecution, which drove those venerable men out of the Church, and with which Queen Elizabeth's Clergy were as deeply tinctured as ever Queen Mary's were; secondly, at the weakness of those holy confessors, many of whom spent so much of their time and strength, in disputing about surplices and hoods, or kneeling at the Lord's Supper!

My will is made. What have I more to do, but to commend my soul to my merciful and faithful Creator?

O what will not those either believe or assert, who are resolved to defend a desperate cause!

Some will not hear even the word of God out of a church, for the sake of these we are often permitted to preach in a church.

I reduced the sixteen Stewards to seven; to whom were given the following instructions:

1. You are to be men full of the Holy Ghost and wisdom, that you may do all things in a manner acceptable to God.

2. You are to be present every Tuesday and Thursday morning, in order to transact the temporal affairs of the Society.

3. You are to begin and end every Meeting with earnest prayer unto God, for a blessing on all your undertakings.

4. You are to produce your accounts the first Tuesday in every month, that they may be transcribed into the ledger.

5. You are to take it in turn, month by month, to be chairman. The chairman is to see that all the rules be punctually observed, and immediately to check him who breaks any of them.

6. You are to do nothing without the consent of the Minister, either actually had, or reasonably presumed.

7. You are to consider, whenever you meet, "God is here." Therefore, be deeply serious. Utter no trifling word. Speak as in his presence, and to the glory of his great name.

8. When anything is debated, let one at once stand up and speak, the rest giving attention; and let him speak just loud enough to be heard, in love and the spirit of meekness.

9. You are continually to pray, and endeavour that a holy harmony of soul may in all things subsist among you; that in every step you may

keep the unity of the Spirit in the bond of peace.

10. In all debates, you are to watch over your spirits, avoiding as fire all clamour and contention, being swift to hear, slow to speak; in honour every man preferring another before himself.

11. If you cannot relieve, do not grieve the poor. Give them soft words, if nothing else. Abstain from either sour looks or harsh words. Let them be glad to come, even though they should go empty away. Put yourself in the place of every poor man, and deal with him as you would God should deal with you.

I procured a genuine account of the great Irish massacre in 1641. Surely never was there such a transaction before, from the beginning of the world! More than two hundred thousand men, women and children, butchered within a few months in cold blood, and with such circumstances of cruelty as make one's blood run cold! It is well if God has not a controversy with the nation, on this very account, to this day.

I began examining the Society . . . many of whom appeared to be strong in faith. The people in general are of a more teachable spirit than in most parts of England; but on that very account they must be watched over with the more care, being equally susceptible of good and ill impressions.

If we look into a dark pit it seems deep; but

the darkness only makes it seem so. Bring the light and we shall see it is very shallow.

Alas! what a method of conversion is this? I love the Church too; but I would no more starve men into the Church, than burn them into it.

Let us make a conscience of magnifying or exaggerating any thing. Let us rather speak under than above the truth. We, of all men, should be punctual in all we say, that none of our words may fall to the ground.

Indeed almost all the town appeared to be moved, full of good-will and desires of salvation. But the waters spread too wide to be deep of salvation.

But still they who are ready to eat up every word, do not appear ready to digest any part of it.

But his [St. Patrick's] success staggers me the most of all: no blood of the martyrs is here; no reproach, no scandal of the cross; no persecution to those that will live godly. Nothing is to be heard of from the beginning to the end, but kings, nobles, warriors, bowing down before him. Thousands are converted, without any opposition at all: twelve thousand at one sermon. If these things were so, either there was then no Devil in the world, or St. Patrick did not preach the Gospel of Christ.

I see plainly we have often judged amiss, when we have measured the increase of the work of God, in this and other places, by the increase of the Society only. The Society here is not large, but God has wrought upon the whole place: sabbath-breaking and drunkenness are no more seen in these streets; cursing and swearing are rarely heard. Wickedness hides its head already; who knows but by and by God may utterly take it away?

One of my old companions returned, my headache, which I never had while I abstained from animal food.

And all this time you were talking of justice and law! Alas, Sir, suppose we were Dissenters (which I deny), suppose we were Jews or Turks, are we not to have the benefit of the laws of our country? Proceed against us by the law, if you can or dare, but not by lawless violence.

So clear it is, that love will not always prevail; but there is a time for the terrors of the Lord.

The more I converse with this people, the more I am amazed . . . It is plain, God begins his work at the heart; then the inspiration of the highest giveth understanding.

I finished the translation of Martin Luther's Life. Doubtless he was a man highly favoured of God, and a blessed instrument in his hand. But O! what pity that he had no faithful friend!

None that would, at all hazards, rebuke him plainly and sharply, for his rough, untractable spirit and bitter zeal for opinions, so greatly obstructive of the work of God.

Through all Cornwall I find the Societies have suffered great loss from want of discipline. Wisely said the ancients, "The soul and body make a man; the spirit and discipline make a Christian."

For many years I remained single, because I believed I could be more useful in a single, than in a married state. And I praise God, who enabled me so to do. I now as fully believe, that in my present circumstances I might be more useful in a married state.

I met the single men, and showed them on how many accounts it was good for those who had received that gift from God, to remain single for the kingdom of heaven's sake, unless where a particular case might be an exception to the general rule.

I cannot understand how a Methodist Preacher can answer it to God, to preach one Sermon, or travel one day less, in a married, than in a single state. In this respect, surely "it remaineth that they who have wives be as though they had none."

Since he has known the pardoning love of

God, he has been swiftly going on from faith to faith, and growing not in knowledge only, but in love.

Hath not God the hearts of all men in his hand? Who would have expected to see me preaching in Wakefield Church to so attentive a congregation, a few years ago, when all the people were as roaring lions, and the honest man did not dare to let me preach in his yard, lest the mob should pull down his house? . . . All is peace here now, since the trial at York; at which the Magistrates were sentenced to rebuild the house, which the mob had pulled down. Surely the Magistrate has been the minister of God to us for good!

The light punishment inflicted on the late rioters . . . has secured peace ever since. Such a mercy it is, to execute the penalty of the law, on those who will not regard its precepts! So many inconveniences to the innocent does it prevent, and so much sin in the guilty.

A huge multitude, rich and poor . . . were soon gathered together. . . . Some thousands of the people seriously attended; but many behaved as if possessed by Moloch. Clods and stones flew about on every side; but they neither touched nor disturbed me. When I had finished my discourse, I went to take coach; but the chachman had driven clear away. We were at a loss, till a gentlewoman invited my wife and me to come into her coach. She brought some inconveniences on herself thereby. . . . The mob, who were increased to several thousands, when I stepped out of the coach into Mr. A's house, perceiving I was escaped out of their hands, revenged themselves on the windows, with many showers of stones, which they poured in, even into the rooms four stories high. Mr. A walked through them to the Mayor's house, who gave him fair words, but no assistance; probably not knowing, that himself (the Mayor) might be compelled to make good all the damage which should be done. He then went in quest of Constables, and brought two with him about nine o'clock. With their help he so thoroughly dispersed the mob, that no two of them were left together.

I find it useful to be in such a state of suspense, wherein I know not what will be the next hour, but lean absolutely on His disposal, who knoweth and ruleth all things well.

If I have any strength at all (and I have none but what I have received), it is in forgiving injuries; and on this very side am I assaulted more frequently than on any other.

I visited one in the Marshalsea Prison, nursery of all manner of wickedness. A shame to man, that there should be such a place, such a picture of hell upon earth! And shame to those who bear the name of Christ, that there should need any prison at all in Christendom!

From Dr. Franklin's Letters I learned: 1. That
electrical fire is a species of fire infinitely finer
than any other yet known. 2. That it is diffused,
and in nearly equal proportions, through almost
all substances. 3. That as long as it is thus diffused, it has no discernible effect. 4. That if any
quantity of it be collected together, whether by
art or nature, it then becomes visible, in the form
of fire, and inexpressibly powerful. 5. That it
is essentially different from the light of the sun;
for it pervades a thousand bodies which light
cannot penetrate, and yet cannot penetrate
glass, which light pervades so freely. 6. That
lightning is no other than the electrical fire collected by one or more clouds. 7. That all the
effects of lightning may be performed by the
artificial electrical fire. 8. That any thing
pointed, as a spire or tree, attracts the lightning,
just as a needle does the electrical fire. 9. That
the electrical fire, discharged on a rat or a fowl
will kill it instantly; but discharged on one
dipped in water, will slide off, and do it no hurt
at all. In like manner, the lightning which will
kill a man in a moment, will not hurt him if
he be thoroughly wet. What an amazing scene
is here opened for after ages to improve upon!

I was surprised to find so little fruit here
(Portsmouth), after so much preaching. That
accursed itch of disputing had well nigh destroyed all the seed which had been sown. And
this vain jangling they called contending for the
faith! I doubt the whole faith of these poor
wretches is but an opinion.

I never saw so many people in this church, nor did I ever before speak so plainly to them. They hear; but when will they feel? O what can man do toward raising either dead bodies or dead souls?

I willingly accepted the offer of preaching in the house lately built for Mr. Whitefield, at Plymouth Dock. Thus it behoveth us to trample on bigotry and party zeal. Ought not all who love God to love one another?

I was sent for by one of my neighbours, dying of consumption. She seemed full of good desires; but who does not, when death stands at the door?

In my hours of walking I read Dr. Calamy's abridgment of Mr. Baxter's *Life*. What a scene is opened here. In spite of all the prejudice of education, I could not but see that the poor Nonconformists had been used without either justice or mercy; and that many of the Protestant Bishops of King Charles, had neither more religion nor humanity than the Popish Bishops of Queen Mary.

I preached at Sadler's Wells, in what was formerly a playhouse. I am glad when it pleases God to take possession of what Satan esteemed his own ground. The place, though large, was extremely crowded; and deep attention sat on every face.

I preached at Charlton, a village six miles from Taunton, to a large congregation, gathered from the towns and country, for many miles round. All the farmers here had, some time before, entered into a joint engagement, "To turn all out of their service, and give no work to any who went to hear a Methodist Preacher"; but there is no counsel against the Lord. One of the chief of them . . . was not long after convinced of the truth, and desired those very men to preach at his house. Many of the other confederates came to hear, whom their servants . . . gladly followed; so the whole device of Satan fell to the ground, and the word of God grew and prevailed.

Oct. 28, 1754

Sir,

Whether I see you any more in this life or not, I rejoice that I have seen you this once, and that God enabled you to bear with patience what I spoke in the simplicity of my heart.

The substance of what I took the liberty to mention to you this morning was: You are on the borders of the grave, as well as I; shortly we must both appear before God. When it seemed to me, some months since, that my life was near an end, I was troubled that I had not dealt plainly with you. This you will permit me to do now, without any reserve, in the fear and in the presence of God.

I reverence you for your office as a magistrate: I believe you to be an honest, upright man; I

love you for having protected an innocent people from their cruel and lawless oppressors: but
so much the more am I obliged to say (though
I judge not, God is the judge), I fear you are
covetous, that you love the world: and if you
do, as sure as the word of God is true, you are
not in a state of salvation.

The substance of your answer was, that many
people exhort others to charity from self-interest; that men of fortune must mind their fortune; that you cannot go about to look for poor
people; that when you have seen them yourself,
and relieved them, they were scarce ever satisfied; that many make an ill use of what you
give them; that you cannot trust the account
people give of themselves by letters; that nevertheless, you do give to private persons by the
hands of others; that you have also given to
several hospitals . . . but that you must support
your family; . . . that you are for great things,
for public charities, and for saving the nation
from ruin. . . .

To this I replied: 1. Sir, I have no self-interest
in this matter; . . . but I am concerned for your
immortal spirit . . . 2. It is true men of fortune
must mind their fortune, but they must not love
the world . . . 3. It is true, likewise, you cannot
go about to look for poor people, but you may
be sufficiently informed of them by those that
can. 4. And if some of these are never satisfied,
this is no reason for not relieving others. 5. Suppose, too, that some make an ill use of what
you give, the loss falls on their own head. You

will not lose your reward for their fault. What you laid out, God will pay you again. 6. Yet certainly you do well to have all the assurance you can, that those to whom you give, are likely to make a good use of it . . . 7. I rejoice that you have given to many . . . 8. I rejoice likewise, that you have given some hundreds of pounds to the hospitals, and wish it had been ten thousand. 9. To the support of the family I did not object; but begged leave to ask, whether this could not be done without giving ten thousand a year to one who had as much already? And, whether you could answer this to God in the day wherein he shall judge the world? 10. I likewise granted, that the family had continued above four hundred years, but . . . that God regarded it not a jot the more for this; . . . 11. I observed . . . that great things may be done, and little things left undone. 12. And that if this, or any other way of thinking, be according to Scripture, then it is sound and good . . . As to yourself, you are not the proprietor of any thing, no, not of one shilling in the world: you are only a steward of what another entrusts you with . . . not according to your will, but his . . . 2. Is not God the sole proprietor of all things? And are not you to give an account to him for every part of his goods? 3. Is not death at hand? Are we not just going to appear in the presence of God, and that naked of all worldly goods? Will you then rejoice in the money you have left behind you? . . . for the sake of your immortal soul, examine yourself, whether you do not love money? If so, you cannot love God. And if we die without the fear of God, what remains? Only to be banished from Him for ever and ever!

I am, with true respect, Sir,

Your servant for Christ's sake.

There is a solid serious people in these parts, who stand their ground against all opposition. The warmest opposers are the Jacobites, who do not love us, because we love King George: but they profit nothing; for more and more people "fear God, and honour the King."

We rode in less than four hours the eight miles to Newell-Hay. Just as I began to preach, the sun broke out, and shone exceeding hot on the side of my head. I found, if it continued, I should not be able to speak long, and lifted up my heart to God. In a minute or two it was covered with clouds, which continued till the service was over. Let any who please, call this chance: I call it an answer to prayer.

At three in the afternoon I preached at Heptonstall, on the brow of the mountain. The rain began almost as soon as I began to speak. I prayed that, if God saw best, it might be stayed till I had delivered his word. It was so, and then began again: but we had only a short stage to Ewood.

In the afternoon I was obliged to go out of the church, abundance of people not being able

to get in. The rain ceased, from the moment I
came out, till I had finished my discourse. How
many proofs must we have, that there is no
petition too little, any more than too great, for
God to grant!

We began reading together, "A Gentleman's
Reasons for his Dissent from the Church of
England." It is an elaborate and lively Tract,
and contains the strength of the cause; but it
did not yield us one proof that it is lawful for
us . . . to separate from it.

Here likewise was such a number of people
assembled as was never before seen in that
town. Is not this one clear proof of the hand
of God, that although the novelty of this preaching is over, yet the people flock to hear it in every
place, far more than when it was a new thing.

I was considering, what could be the reasons
why the hand of the Lord (who does nothing
without a cause) is almost entirely stayed in
Scotland, and in great measure in New England?
It does not become us to judge peremptorily,
but perhaps some of them may be these: 1. Many
of them became wise in their own eyes: they
seemed to think they were the men, and there
were none like them; and hence they refused
God the liberty of sending by whom He would
send, and required Him to work by men of
learning, or not at all. 2. Many of them were
bigots, immoderately attached either to their

own opinions or mode of worship. . . . Hence they not only suffered in themselves and their brethren a bitter zeal, but applauded themselves therein . . . 3. With pride, bitterness and bigotry, self-indulgence was joined; self-denial was little taught and practised. . . . No marvel then, that the spirit of God was grieved. Let us profit by their example.

I was much affected about this time, by a letter sent from a gentleman in Virginia. Part of it runs thus:

"The poor negro slaves here never heard of Jesus, or his religion, till they arrived at the land of their slavery in America; whom their masters generally neglect, as though immortality was not the privilege of their souls, in common with their own. These poor Africans are the principal objects of my compassion, and, I think, the most proper subject of your charity.

"The inhabitants of Virginia are computed to be about 300,000, and the one-half of them are supposed to be negroes. The number of these who attend on my ministry, at particular times, is uncertain; but I think there are about three hundred who give a stated attendance. And never have I been so much struck with the appearance of an assembly, as when I have glanced my eye on one part of the house, adorned . . . with so many black countenances, eagerly attentive to every word they heard, and some of them covered with tears. A considerable number of them, about a hundred, have been baptized, after they had been fully instructed in the great truths of religion, and had evidenced their sense of them by a life of the strictest virtue. As they are not sufficiently polished to dissemble with a good grace, they express the sensations of their hearts so much in the language of simple nature, and with such genuine indications of artless sincerity, that it is impossible to suspect their professions, especially when attended with a suitable behavior.

"Mr. Todd, Minister of the next congregation, has near the same number under his care; and several of them also . . . discover the same seriousness. Indeed there are multitudes of them in various parts, who are eagerly desirous of instruction. They have generally very little help to read; and yet, to my agreeable surprise, sundry of them, by dint of application, in their very few leisure hours, have made such a progress, that they are able to read their Bible, or a plain author, very intelligibly. But few of their masters will be at the expense of furnishing them with books. I have supplied them to the utmost of my ability. They are exceedingly delighted with Watts Songs. And I cannot but observe, that the Negroes, above all of the human species I ever knew, have the nicest ear for music. They have a kind of ecstatic delight in psalmody: nor are there any books they so soon learn, or take so much pleasure in, as those used in that heavenly part of divine worship."

I received a remarkable letter, part of which I have here subjoined:

. . . "Can it be, that the great God of the boundless universe, containing many thousand better worlds than this, should become incarnate here, and die on a piece of wood? There I lose my belief of Christianity.

"But on the other hand, I think, well, let me examine the fitness of things which Deism boasts of; and certain it is, I discern nothing but beauty and wisdom in the inanimate parts of the creation: but how is the animate side of nature? It shocks me with powerful cruelty, and bleeding innocence. I cannot call the earth . . . 'A great rolling globe, covered over with fools'; but rather, a great rolling globe, covered over with slaughter-houses, where few beings can escape but those of the butcher kind, the lion, wolf, or tiger: and, as to man himself, he is undoubtedly the supreme lord, nay, the uncontrollable tyrant, of this globe. Yet survey him in a state of Deism, and I must pronounce him a very poor creature; he is then a kind of jack-ketch, and executioner-general. He may, nay he must, destroy, for his own subsistence, multitudes of beings that have done him no wrong. He has none of that heavenly power to restore life: and can he be fond of the permission to take it away? One who, like me, is subject to the tender passions, will never be proud of this. The very beasts are entitled to my compassion; but who can express the anxieties I feel for the afflictions sustained by virtuous men, and my abhorrence of the cruel? Yet in Deism, I can discern no reward for the one, or punishment for the other. On this view of things, the Castilian King might well say, 'He could have directed God to amend his creation.'

"I think upon the whole, the God of wisdom would not have made a world so much in want of a Redeemer as this, and not give it one; therefore, at present, I am again a Christian. O that the son of God would confirm me his!"

I was in the robe-chamber, adjoining to the House of Lords, when the King put on his robes. His brow was much furrowed with age, and quite clouded with care. And is this all the world can give even to a King? All the grandeur it can afford? A blanket of ermine round his shoulders, so heavy and cumbersome he can scarce move under it! A huge heap of borrowed hair, with a few plates of gold and glittering stones upon his head! Alas, what a bauble is human greatness! And even this will not endure.

But still he disputed, whether any man should pray to Christ. I gave these reasons for it: 1. All men are bound to *honour* the Son, *as they honour the Father;* but we are to honour the Father, by praying to him; therefore we should so honour the Son . . . for what is "to call upon His name," but to pray to Him?

When he could not answer these reasons, he called them cant. . . . What he calls "contempt," was confronting him with Scripture and reason, in defense of the Godhead of Christ. . . . It grieves me to see the people led in the high road to hell instead of heaven; especially at a time which calls upon all to awake and "prepare to meet their God."

In returning to London, I read the life of the late Czar, Peter the Great. Undoubtedly he was a Soldier, a General and a Statesman, scarce inferior to any; but why was he called a Christian? What has Christianity to do either with deep dissimulation or savage cruelty?

I received the copy of another letter from the Rev. Mrs. Davies, in Virginia, part of which I have subjoined:

"When the books arrived, I gave public notice after sermon, and desired such negroes as could read, and such white people as would make good use of them, and were not able to buy, to come to my house. For some time after, the poor slaves, whenever they could get an hour's leisure, hurried away to me, and received them with all the genuine indication of passionate gratitude. All the books were very acceptable, but none more so than the Psalms and Hymns, which enabled them to gratify their peculiar taste for psalmody. Sundry of them lodged all night in my kitchen; and sometimes when I have awakened, at two or three in the morning, a torrent of sacred psalmody has poured into my chamber. In this exercise some of them spend the whole night.

"The good effects of this charity are already apparent. It convinces the heathen, that however careless about religion the generality of the white people are, yet there are some who think it a matter of importance. It has excited some of their masters to emulation, and they are ashamed that strangers on the other side of the Atlantic Ocean, should be at such pains to teach their domestics, while themselves are negligent about it. Such of the negroes as can read already, are evidently improving in knowledge. It has excited others to learn to read; for as I give books to none but such as can read, they consider them as a reward for their industry: and I am told, that in almost every house in my congregation, and in many other places, they spend every leisure hour in endeavouring to learn. Many do this from a sincere desire to know the will of God; and if some should do it from meaner principle of vanity or curiosity, yet I cannot but rejoice that it renders them the more capable of receiving instruction. To all this I may add, that the very distributing of these books gives me an opportunity of speaking seriously, and with particular application, to many who would not otherwise come in my way.

"Two Sundays ago I had the pleasure of seeing forty of their black faces at the Lord's Table,

several of whom give unusual evidence of their
sincerity in religion. Last Sunday I baptized
seven or eight, who had been catechized for
some time. Indeed many of them appear determined to press into the kingdom, and I am persuaded will find an abundant entrance, when
many of the children of the kingdom are shut
out."

But how is it, that almost in every place, even
where there is not lasting fruit, there is so great
an impression made at first, upon a considerable
number of people? The fact is this: everywhere
the work of God rises higher and higher, till it
comes to a point. Here it seems for a short time
to be at a stay; and then it gradually sinks again.

All this may easily be accounted for. At first
curiosity brings many hearers: at the same time
God draws many by his preventing grace to hear
his Word, and comforts them in hearing. One
then tells another. By this means, on the one
hand, curiosity spreads and increases, and on
the other, drawings of God's Spirit touch more
hearts, and many of them more powerfully than
before. He now offers grace to all that hear,
desire to please God, and good-will to his mes-
senger; these principles variously combined and
increasing, raise the general work to its highest
point. But it cannot stand here; for, in the nature
of things, curiosity must soon decline. Again,
the drawings of God are not followed, and
thereby the Spirit of God is grieved. The consequence is, he strives with this and this man

no more, and so his drawings end. Thus both
the natural and supernatural power declining,
most of the hearers will be less and less affected.
Add to this, that in the process of the work "it
must be, that offences will come." Some of the
hearers, if not Preachers also, will act contrary
to their profession. Either their follies or faults
will be told from one to another, and lose nothing in the telling. Men once curious to hear, will
now draw back: men once drawn, having stifled
their good desires, will disapprove what they
approved before, and feel dislike, instead of
good-will, to the Preacher. Others, who were
more or less convinced, will be afraid or
ashamed to acknowledge that conviction. . . .
When by this means, all who do not savingly
believe, have quenched the Spirit of God, the
little flock goes on from faith to faith; the rest
sleep on and take their rest. And thus the
number of hearers in every place may be expected first to increase and then decrease.

Does not experience show the sad effects of
a contrary education? While children, instead
of being taught benevolence to irrationals, are
suffered to torment first poor little insects, and
then every helpless creature that comes in their
way; can it be expected that, being thus inured
to cruelty and oppression even in their tender
years they should relent when they come to age,
and be susceptible of compassion, even to ratio-
nals? It cannot, for is pity shown to man only
because he has reason? If so, those would lose

their claim to our compassion, who stand in the greatest need of it, namely, children, idiots and lunatics: but if pity is shown to all that are capable of pain, then may it justly be expected that we should sympathize with every thing that has life.

I am persuaded you are not insensible of the pain given to every Christian, every humane heart, by those savage diversions, bull-baiting, cock-fighting, horse-racing and hunting. Can any of these irrational and unnatural sports appear otherwise than cruel, unless through early prejudice, or entire want of consideration and reflection? And if man is void of these, does he deserve the name of man, or is he fit for society? And besides, how dreadful are the concomitant and the consequent vices of these savage routs? Yet such cowards are we grown, that scarce any man has courage to draw his pen against them!

Wednesday and Thursday I settled my temporal business. It is now about eighteen years since I began writing and printing books. And how much in that time have I gained by printing? Why, on summing up my accounts, I found . . . I had gained by printing and preaching together, a debt of twelve hundred and thirty-six pounds.

I received the following letter:

"As it is our duty to do all we can to make all round us happy, I think there is one thing that may be done to promote so blessed an end, which will at the same time be very advantageous to them that practise it; namely, to efface all the obscene words which are written on houses, doors, or walls, by evil-minded men. This, which I recommend to others, I constantly practise myself; and if ever I omit doing it, I am severely checked, unless I can produce some good reason for that omission. I do it with a sponge which, for that purpose, I carry in my pocket. The advantages I reap from hence are: 1. Peace of conscience in doing my duty: 2. It helps me to conquer the fear of man, which is one of my greatest trials: 3. It is matter of joy, that I can do any the least service to any one. And as all persons, especially the young, are liable to temptations of impurity, I cannot do too much to remove such temptations, either from myself or others. Perhaps too, when the unhappy writers pass by, and see their bad labours soon effaced, they may be discouraged from pursuing so shameful a work, yea, and brought to a better mind.

"Perhaps in some places it might not be amiss, in the room of what is effaced, to write some serious sentence, or short text of Scripture: and wherever we do this, would it not be well to lift up our heart to God, in behalf of those sinners, in this or the like manner, 'Lord, lay not this sin to their charge: Father, forgive them, for they know not what they do.'"

Having procured an apparatus on purpose, I ordered several persons to be electrified, who were ill of various disorders; some of whom

found an immediate, some a gradual cure. From
this time I appointed, first some hours in every
week, and afterwards an hour in every day,
wherein any that desired it, might try the virtue
of this surprising medicine. Two or three years
after, our patients were so numerous, that we
were obliged to divide them.

I visited a poor dying back-slider, full of good
resolutions: but who can tell, when these imply
a real change of heart, and when they do not;
when they spring from fear only, what will they
avail before God?

In the evening the tent (so they call a covered
pulpit) was placed in the yard of the poor-house,
a very large and commodious place. Fronting
the pulpit was the infirmary, with most of the
patients at or near the windows. Adjoining to
this was the hospital for lunatics; several of
them gave deep attention. And cannot God give
them also the spirit of a sound mind?

I took a walk in the Charter-House. I won-
dered that all the squares and buildings, and
especially the school-boys, looked so little. But
this is easily accounted for. I was little myself
when I was at school, and measured all about
me by myself. Accordingly, the upper boys being
then bigger than myself, seemed to me very big
and tall; quite contrary to what they appear
now, when I am taller and bigger than them.
I question if this is not the real ground of the

common imagination, that our forefathers, and in general men in past ages, were much larger than now; an imagination current in the world eighteen hundred years ago. . . . Whereas in reality men have been, at least ever since the deluge, very nearly the same as we find them now, both for stature and understanding.

A few days ago, some hundred English, who had been prisoners in France, were landed at Penzance by a cartel ship. Many of these passed through Redruth, going home; but in a most forlorn condition. None showed more compassion to them than the French. They gave them food, clothes, or money, and told them, "We wish we could do more; but we have little for ourselves here." Several who had only two shirts, gave a naked Englishman one. A French boy meeting an English boy who was half naked, took hold of him, and stopped him, cried over him a while, and then pulled off his own coat and put it upon him!

In the evening I met all the married men and women of the Society. I believe it was high time; for many of them seemed to know very little of relative duties; so that I brought strange things to their ears, when I enlarged on the duties of husbands, and wives, and parents.

I preached at eight, and at five, Afterward I was desired to make a collection for a distressed family. Mr. Booker, the Minister of the parish,

willingly stood at the door to receive it; and
encouraged all that went by to be "merciful after
their powers."

. . . there is no folly too great even for a man
of sense, if he resolve to follow his own imagination!

How unspeakable is the advantage in point
of common sense, which middling people have
over the rich! There is so much paint and affec-
tation, so many unmeaning words and senseless
customs, among people of rank.

I rode back . . . in order to put the Society
there (an unlicked mass) into some form. This
on Saturday they had begged me to do; but (on
Tuesday) they seemed now to have quite forgotten it . . . the Presbyterian Minister had turned
them upside down. They looked as if they had
never seen me before; all but five or six, who
were much ashamed of their brethren.

I rode to Wandsworth, and baptized two negroes belonging to Mr. Gilbert, a gentleman
lately come from Antigua. One of these is deeply
convinced of sin; the other rejoices in God her
Savior, and is the first African Christian I have
known. But shall not our Lord, in due time, have
these Heathens also "for his inheritance?"

I found the Society had decreased . . . and
yet they had had full as good Preachers; but

that is not sufficient. By repeated experiments we learn, that though a man preach like an angel, he will neither collect nor preserve a Society which is collected, without visiting them from house to house.

Lodging with a sensible man, I inquired particularly into the present discipline of the Scotch parishes. In one parish, it seems, there are twelve ruling Elders; in another there are fourteen. And what are these? Men of great sense and deep experience? Neither one nor the other. But they are the richest men in the parish. And are the richest of course the best and the wisest men? Does the Bible teach this? I fear not. What manner of governors then will these be? Why, they are generally just as capable of governing a parish as of commanding an army.

I had hardly finished the hymn, when I observed the people in great confusion, which was occasioned by a Lieutenant of a man-of-war, who had chosen that time to bring his press-gang, and ordered them to take Joseph Jones and William Alwood. Joseph Jones telling him, "Sir, I belong to Mr. Wesley," after a few words, he let him go; as he did likewise William Alwood, after a few hours, understanding he was a licensed Preacher. He likewise seized upon a young man of the town; but the women rescued him by main strength. They also broke the Lieutenant's head, and so stoned both him and his men, that they ran away with all speed.

. . . a large congregation was waiting; and all behaved well, but an honest tar, who was much distressed, at my saying, "No man is delivered from the fear of death, but he that fears God."

Accordingly, the next evening, after sermon, I reminded them of two things: the one, that it was not decent to begin talking aloud as soon as service was ended, and hurrying to and fro, as in a beer-garden; the other, that it was a bad custom to gather into knots just after sermon, and turn a place of worship into a coffee-house. I therefore desired, that none would talk under that roof, but go quietly and silently away. And on Sunday . . . I had the pleasure to observe, that all went as quietly away, as if they had been accustomed to it for many years.

The next day . . . I read Mr. Huygen's "Conjectures on the Planetary World." He surprised me. I think he clearly proves that the moon is not habitable. . . . That there is no sea, no water on her surface, nor any atmosphere; and hence he very rationally infers, that "neither are the secondary planets inhabited." And who can prove that the primary are? I know the earth is: of the rest I know nothing.

The danger was to regard extraordinary circumstances too much, such as outcries, convulsions, visions, trances, as if these were essential to the inward work, so that it could not go on without them. Perhaps the danger is to retard them too little; to condemn them altogether; to imagine they had nothing of God in them, and were a hindrance to his work. Whereas the truth is: 1. God suddenly and strongly convinced many that they were lost sinners; the natural consequence whereof were sudden outcries, and strong bodily convulsions: 2. To strengthen and encourage them that believed, and to make his work more apparent, he favoured several of them with divine dreams, others with trances and visions: 3. In some of these instances, after a time, nature mixed with grace: 4. Satan likewise mimicked this work of God, in order to discredit the whole work; and yet it is not wise to give up this part, any more than to give up the whole. At first it was doubtless wholly from God. It is partly so at this day. And he will enable us to discern how far, in every case, the work is pure, and where it mixes, or degenerates.

Let us even suppose, that in some few cases, there was a mixture of dissimulation; that persons pretended to see or feel what they did not, and imitated the cries or convulsive motions of those who were really overpowered by the Spirit of God; yet even this should not make us either deny or undervalue the real work of the Spirit. The shadow is no disparagement of the substance, nor the counterfeit of the real diamond.

Our Church requires that Clergymen should be men of learning, and to this end have a university education; but how many have a university education and yet no learning at all? Yet

these men are ordained! Meantime one of emi-
nent learning as well as unblameable behavior,
cannot be ordained, "because he was not at the
university!" What a mere farce is this? Who
would believe that any Christian Bishop would
stoop to so poor an evasion?

To candid . . . men, I am not afraid to lay
open what have been the inmost thoughts of
my heart. . . . I am a creature of a day, passing
through life as an arrow through the air. I am
a spirit come from God, and returning to God
. . . a few moments hence, I am no more seen;
I drop into an unchangeable eternity! I want to
know one thing . . . the way to heaven; how
to land safe on that happy shore. God Himself
has condescended to teach the way; for this very
end He came from heaven. He hath written it
down in a book. O give me that book! At any
price, give me the book of God!

There are four grand and powerful arguments
which strongly induce us to believe that the
Bible must be from God, viz., miracles, prophecies, the goodness of the doctrine, and the moral
character of the penmen. All the miracles come
from divine power; all the prophecies, from divine understanding; the goodness of the doctrine, from divine goodness; and the moral character of the penman, from divine holiness.

The general rule of interpreting Scripture is
this: the literal sense of every text is to be taken,

if it be not contrary to some other texts; but in that case the obscure text is to be interpreted by those which speak more plainly.

The Christian rule of right and wrong is the Word of God, the writings of the Old and New Testament. . . .

This is a lantern unto a Christian's feet, and a light in all his paths. This alone he receives as his rule of right or wrong, of whatever is good or evil . . . . Whatever the Scripture neither forbids nor enjoins . . . he believes to be of an indifferent nature; to be in itself neither good nor evil; this being the whole and sole outward rule whereby his conscience is to be directed in all things.

The Spirit of God, not only once inspired those who wrote it, but continually inspires, supernaturally assists those that read it with earnest prayer.

If you desire to read the Scriptures . . . most effectually . . . would it not be advisable: (1) To set apart a little time, if you can, every morning and evening for that purpose? (2) At each time . . . to read a chapter out of the Old, and one out of the New Testament; if you cannot do this, to take a single chapter, or a part of one? (3) To read this with a single eye, to know the whole will of God, and a fixed resolution to do it? (4) Have a constant eye to the analogy of faith, the connexion and harmony there is

between those grand, fundamental doctrines,
original sin, justification by faith, the new birth,
inward and outward holiness: (5) Serious and
earnest prayer should be constantly used before
we consult the oracles of God. . . . Our reading
should likewise be closed with prayer . . . (6)
It might also be of use . . . to pause, and examine
ourselves by what we read, both with regard
to our hearts and lives.

God has made men the immediate instruments
of all [Divine] revelations, so evangelical faith
must be partly founded on human testimony.
By men were both the Old and New Testament
wrote: and if we consider them abstracted from
their Divine authority, they must be allowed to
be of equal credibility, at least, with all other
ancient writings.

Christianity requires our assent to nothing,
but what is plain and intelligible in every proposition. Let every man first have a full conviction
of the truth of each proposition in the gospel,
as far only as it is plain and intelligible, and
let him believe as far as he understands.

The Son of God begins his work in man by
enabling us to believe in him. He both opens
and enlightens the eyes of our understanding.

The desire of knowledge is an universal principle in man, fixed in his inmost nature. . . .
But although our desire of knowledge has no

bounds, yet our knowledge itself has. It is, indeed, confined within very narrow bounds; abundantly narrower than common people imagine, or men of learning are willing to acknowledge: A strong intimation (since the great Creator doeth nothing in vain), that there will be some future state of being, wherein that now insatiable desire will be satisfied, and there will no longer be so immense a distance between the appetite and the object of it.

Let reason do all that reason can: Employ it as far as it will go. But, at the same time, acknowledge it is utterly incapable of giving either faith, or hope, or love; and, consequently, of producing either real virtue, or substantial happiness.

What Christianity promised is accomplished in my soul. And Christianity, considered as an inward principle, is the completion of all those promises. It is holiness and happiness, the image of God impressed on a created spirit, a fountain of peace and love springing up into the everlasting life . . . and this I conceive to be the strongest evidence of the truth of Christianity.

The world around us is the mighty volume wherein God hath declared himself. Human languages and characters are different in different nations. . . . But the book of nature is written in an universal language. It consists not of words, but things which picture out the Divine perfections.

The omnipresence of God is far too vast to be comprehended by the narrow limits of human understanding. We can only say, the great God, the eternal, the almighty Spirit, is as unbounded in his presence, as in his duration and power.

Now, if man be capable of choosing good or evil, then he is a proper object of the justice of God, acquitting or condemning, rewarding or punishing.

The almighty, all-wise God sees and knows, from everlasting to everlasting, all that is, that was, and that is to come, through one eternal *now*. With him nothing is either past or future, but all things equally present.

If [election] be so, then is all preaching vain. It is needless to them that are elected; for they, whether with preaching or without, will infallibly be saved. Therefore, the end of preaching . . . to save souls . . . is void with regard to them; and it is useless to them that are not elected, for they cannot possibly be saved: They, whether with preaching or without, will infallibly be damned. . . .

This, then, is a plain proof that the doctrine of predestination is not a doctrine of God, because it makes void the ordinance of God; and God is not divided against himself.

This doctrine [predestination] tends to destroy the comfort of religion. . . . All the great and

precious promises are lost . . . for they are not
the elect of God.

This uncomfortable doctrine [predestination]
directly tends to destroy our zeal for good
works.

We could not rejoice that there is a God, were
there not a Mediator [Jesus Christ] also; one who
stands between God and men, to reconcile men
to God, and to transact the whole affair of our
salvation. This excludes all other mediators, as
saints and angels, whom the Papists set us, and
idolatrously worship as such; just as the Heathens of old set up many mediators, to pacify
their superior gods.

But it may be observed, that the Son of God
does not destroy the whole work of the devil
in man, as long as he remains in this life. He
does not destroy bodily weakness, sickness, pain
and a thousand infirmities incident to flesh and
blood. He does not destroy all the weakness of
understanding, which is the natural consequence of the soul's dwelling in a corruptible
body. . . . All these are destroyed by death. And
death itself, "the last enemy" of man, shall be
destroyed at the resurrection.

And therefore every man, in order to believe
unto salvation, must receive the Holy Ghost. . . .
The Holy Spirit prepares us for his inward kingdom, by removing the veil from our heart, and
enabling us to know ourselves as we are known

of him; by "convincing us of sin," of our evil nature, our evil tempers, and our evil words and actions; all of which cannot but partake of the corruption of the heart from which they spring.

In the image of God was man made; holy as He that created him is holy; merciful as the Author of all is merciful; perfect as his Father in heaven is perfect. As God is love, so man, dwelling in love, dwelt in God, and God in him. God made him to be an incorruptible picture of the God of glory. . . . He knew not evil in any kind or degree, but was inwardly and outwardly sinless and undefiled.

Man's liberty . . . necessarily included a power of choosing or refusing either good or evil . . . it cannot be doubted, he might mistake evil for good. He was not infallible; therefore, not impeccable. And this unravels the whole difficulty of the grand question . . . "How came evil into the world?"

Salvation begins with what is usually termed (and very properly) preventing grace; including the first wish to please God, the first dawn of light concerning his will, and the first slight transient conviction of having sinned against him. All these imply some tendency toward life; some degree of salvation; the beginning of a deliverance from blind, unfeeling heart, quite insensible of God and the things of God.

Repentance . . . is a thorough conviction of sin . . . a change of heart (and consequently of life) from all sin to all holiness.

Taking the word in a more particular sense, faith is a divine evidence and conviction not only that "God was in Christ, reconciling the world unto Himself," but also that Christ loved *me,* and gave Himself for *me.*

We must love God, before we can be holy at all; this being the root of all holiness. Now we cannot love God, till we know He loves us.

Reason, however cultivated and improved, cannot produce the love of God.

Neither can any man, while he is in a corruptible body, attain to Adamic perfection. . . . He is unable to avoid falling into innumerable mistakes . . . neither can he always think, speak, and act right. Therefore, man, in his present state, can no more attain Adamic than angelic perfection.

The kingdom of heaven, and the kingdom of God, are but two phrases for the same thing. They mean, not barely a future happy state in heaven, but a state to be enjoyed on earth.

It is impossible for any that have it, to conceal the religion of Jesus Christ. . . . Your holiness makes you as conspicuous as the sun in the midst of heaven.

If [a Christian] sees anything which he approves not, it goes not out of his lips, unless to the person concerned, if haply he may gain his brother. So far is he from making the faults or failings of others the matter of his conversation, that of the absent he never does speak at all, unless he can speak well.

Let no man deceive you with vain words; riches and happiness seldom dwell together. Therefore, if you are wise, you will not seek riches for your children by their marriage.

The person in your house that claims your first and nearest attention, is, undoubtedly, your wife; seeing you are to love her, even as Christ hath loved the Church. . . . Next to your wife are your children; immortal spirits whom God hath, for a time, entrusted to your care, that you may train them up in all holiness, and fit them for the enjoyment of God in eternity.

. . . we ought to gain all we can gain [of money], without buying gold too dear, without paying more for it than it is worth. But this it is certain we ought not to do; we ought not to gain money at the expense of life, nor at the expense of our health.

Why . . . do not all physicians consider how far bodily disorders are caused or influenced by the mind, and in those cases which are utterly out of their sphere call in the assistance of a minister; as ministers, when they find the mind disordered by the body, call in the assistance of a physician? . . . It follows, no man can be a thorough physician without being an experienced Christian.

Ministers are still barely instruments in God's hand, and depend entirely as ever on his blessing, to give the increase to their labours. Without this they are nothing; with it, their part is so small, that they hardly deserve to be mentioned. May their hearts and hands be more united! And retaining a due sense of the honour God doeth them in employing them, may they faithfully labour, not as for themselves, but for the great Proprietor of all, till the day come when he will reward them in full proportion to their fidelity and diligence.

Remember! You live . . . for no other purpose than this, that you may know, love, and serve God on earth, and enjoy him to all eternity. . . . Let every affection, and thought, and word, and work, be subordinate to this. Whatever ye desire or fear, whatever ye seek or shun, whatever ye think, speak or do, be it in order to your happiness in God, the sole End, as well as Source, of your being.

In Conclusion

The Reformation which Luther began took different turns in the lives of other leaders. While Luther held sway in Germany, Calvin was to extend the influence of reformers into the affairs of state and commerce. Calvin believed that the State ultimately must yield to the will of God as understood in the Scriptures. He also argued for the booming growth of capitalism, believing that Christian virtues of thrift and industry should be fulfilled in the new age of commerce. Luther, a generation earlier, did not share this salute to the new capitalist adventurers, preferring the simple life of town and country.

Historians have detailed the sad account of conflict and abuse that frequented the meetings of these sixteenth century churchmen. Luther could not accept the doctrines of the Swiss Reformers and many of the Swiss leaders, like Zwingli, and later Calvin, could not abide Luther's view of Holy Communion. Several attempts were made to reconcile these differences, prompted by the Turkish invasion of Europe and the urging of lay Princes. To no avail. The differences were too deep, the personalities too strong, the times too turbulent.

Luther suffered many ailments and afflictions in his later years. His enormous energy and driving force kept him going to the end—which followed a trip to try and patch up some differences between some German counts. He died in his birthplace, surrounded by family and followers and leaving a legacy that circles the globe.

Calvin without the skills of music that belonged to Luther, nor the rugged, massive frame, nevertheless exerted a powerful influence from his base in Geneva. His great disciple and follower, John Knox, was to transplant the Reformation to Scotland and from there it flowed to the New World. Calvinism shaped America, through government, industry, education and a trained clergy.

Two centuries later, John Wesley would rekindle the spark of Christian belief and ignite entire communities with his forceful, fiery evangelistic message. He brought a mood of joy, an emotion of excitement and inspiration to the Christian life that had languished under the Church of England. By the time of his death in 1791, Wesley had crossed oceans and continents for his faith—one that he shared gladly and warmly.

Bibliography

Martin Luther 1483–1546

Bainton, Roland. *Here I Stand*. Nashville: Abingdon-Cokesbury Press.

Dillenberger, John. *Martin Luther*. Garden City: Doubleday & Company, Inc. Anchor Books.

Lindsay, Thomas. *Luther and the German Revolution*. Edinburgh: T. & T. Clark, Publishers.

Luther, Martin. Works. Edited by Jaroslav Pelikan and Helmut T. Lehmann. 55 vols. St. Louis: Concordia Publishing House; and Philadelphia: Fortress Press.

Ross, Estelle. *Martin Luther*. New York: Frederick A. Stokes.

Smith, Preserved. *Life and Letters of Martin Luther*. Boston: Houghton Mifflin Company.

Thiel, Rudolf. *Luther*. Muhlenberg Press.

John Calvin 1509-1564

The Institutes of the Christian Religion. Translated by John Allen. 2 vols. Presbyterian Board of Christian Education. 1932.

A Compend of the Institutes of the Christian Religion. Hugh Thomason Kerr, Jr., editor. Presbyterian Board of Christian Education. 1939.

Keesecker, William F. *A Calvin Treasury*. New York: Harper & Row, Publishers.

Library of Christian Classics. Volumes XXI, XXII, XXIII. Joseph Haroutunian, editor. Philadelphia: The Westminster Press.

McNeill, John T. *The History and Character of Calvinism*. London: Oxford University Press.

Niesel, Wilhelm. *The Theology of Calvin*. Philadelphia: The Westminister Press.

John Wesley 1703–1791

Bready, Wesley J. *England Before and After Wesley.* New York: Harper and Row, Publishers.

Burtner, Robert W. and Chiles, Robert E. *A Compend of John Wesley's Theology.* Nashville: Abingdon Press.

Cell, George C. *The Rediscovery of John Wesley.* New York: Henry Holt.

McConnell, Francis J. *John Wesley.* Nashville: Abingdon-Cokesbury Press.

Sugden, Edward. *Wesley's Standard Sermons.* 2 vols. London: Epworth Press.

Telford, John. *The Letters of John Wesley.* 8 vols. London: Epworth Press.

Wesley, John. *Journal.* 4 vols. Glasgow: University Press.

PIVOT FAMILY READERS

Inexpensive New Editions of Christian Classics... Complete And Unabridged

☐ **ABIDE IN CHRIST** by Andrew Murray. Printed in larger type, on better paper. The famous book in which the author writes about the true meaning of the words "abide in me." Introduction by William J. Petersen, editor of *Eternity Magazine*. (95¢)

☐ **THE PILGRIM'S PROGRESS** by John Bunyan. The journey of one man's soul—an exciting bigger-than-life adventure story and a document of inspiration and faith. Introduction by Donald T. Kauffman, editor-in-chief, *Christian Herald Family Bookshelf*. (95¢)

☐ **GOLD DUST** by Charlotte Yonge. A treasury of thoughts for every day and eternity in this classic written almost one hundred years ago. The only complete, unabridged edition in inexpensive paperback. Special introduction by William J. Petersen. (95¢)

☐ **OF THE IMITATION OF CHRIST** by Thomas à Kempis. The most famous book of devotion in Christendom, first published in 1418. Now, printed in larger type, on better paper, with special introduction by William J. Petersen. (95¢)

☐ **IN HIS STEPS** by Charles Sheldon. For one year, the members of the First Church have pledged that they will live according to the teachings of Jesus. The most popular novel ever written with a new introduction by Donald T. Kauffman. (95¢)

☐ **KEPT FOR THE MASTER'S USE** by Frances Ridley Havergal. Twelve paths to participation in Gods' mighty promise. The only complete unabridged edition in inexpensive paperback. Special introduction by William J. Petersen. (95¢)

Buy them at your local bookstore or use this handy coupon

THREE VOLUMES IN ONE...
NEVER BEFORE IN PAPERBACK

The Pivot INSPIRATION THREE LIBRARY

brings you the best of inspirational thought together in new, bargain-priced volumes for family enrichment. The larger type and convenient size, the choice of the best authors and selections, make each volume a shared adventure in wisdom and insight for young and old.

☐ **Volume One** contains **As A Man Thinketh** by James Allen; **Acres of Diamonds** by Russell Conwell; and **Essay on Self-Reliance** by Ralph Waldo Emerson. Special introduction by David Poling. ($1.25)

☐ **Volume Two** contains **The Greatest Thing In The World** by Henry Drummond; **The Song Of Our Syrian Guest** by William Allen Knight; and **The Practice Of The Presence of God** by Brother Lawrence. Special introduction by David Poling. ($1.25)

☐ **Volume Three** contains three original anthologies of classic Christian thought: **The Wisdom of Martin Luther; The Wisdom of John Wesley; The Wisdom of John Calvin.** Selected and with a special introduction by David Poling. ($1.25) *Other volumes to be announced shortly*

Buy them at your bookstore or use this handy coupon